THE ART OF CARVING NETSUKE

THE ART OF CARVING NETSUKE

PETER BENSON

Guild of Master
Craftsman Publications

First published 2010 by
Guild of Master Craftsman Publications Ltd
Castle Place, 166 High Street, Lewes,
East Sussex BN7 1XU

ISBN: 978-1-86108-682-2

A catalogue record for this book is available from the British Library.

Associate Publisher: Jonathan Bailey
Production Manager: Jim Bulley
Managing Editor: Gerrie Purcell
Editor: Beth Wicks
Managing Art Editor: Gilda Pacitti
Designer: Rob Janes
Photography: Peter Benson and Anthony Bailey

Colour origination by **GMC Reprographics**
Printed and bound in China by **Hung Hing**

Contents

Introduction

Although there are many books on netsuke, they are primarily aimed at collectors and admirers; there is very little on offer for carvers. The main reason I wrote this book was to redress this issue and to encourage more carvers to experiment with what netsuke carving has to offer.

The book is not intended to be an informed instructional manual for aspiring professional netsuke carvers. My aim is simply to provide enough information and encouragement to get you started on a new way of carving and to help you gain experience in carving miniature pieces. With luck, some of you will go on to produce your own exquisite work, typical of the traditional netsuke carvers, the *netsuke-shi's*.

Why carve netsuke?

There are many practical reasons for carving miniature pieces in general and netsuke pieces in particular. Not only is it a carving experience, but it is also an emotional one. Each piece has its own character that can be humorous or with a slight barb to it, affectionate, historical, mythical, even erotic. The possibilities are almost limitless.

The greatest attraction for me personally has always been the fascination in carving at such small sizes. It is almost like producing my own miniature world. Storage of the finished items is not a problem as a small cabinet can store several years' work.

As the materials are usually only about 2–3in^3 (5–7.5cm^3) in volume, costs are frequently negligible. Consequently, you have a much greater choice of materials. If you decide to work in wood, for example, you have the advantage of being able to choose almost any species as long as it has a fine grain.

With the high costs of timber today and the difficulty in getting hold of many of the more exotic kinds, the fact that you only need a small piece is definitely beneficial. Much of my own work is completed just using a small piece of wood and a scalpel. You also have the opportunity to work with more exotic materials such as ivory, horn, or even tagua nuts.

Other advantages include the minimal mess that carving at such a small scale creates, as well as the flexibility of being able to carve almost anywhere. All your equipment is eminently portable and can therefore be used at any suitable location. Indeed, your tools are very small and can simply be carried around in your pocket.

Netsuke can even be carved in the comfort of your own living room. I have never held with the idea that where there is no pain, there is no gain. If I can carve in comfort, so much the better. There is no substitute for a nice comfortable armchair.

Creativity

Many carvers believe that they have very little, if any, creative talent. Instead, they rely heavily on recreating other people's designs or working from photographs and drawings without progressing onto their own designs. This is, of course, nonsense. We all have the ability to be creative, even though we often lack the subject knowledge or confidence to 'go it alone'.

I recommend using patterns and copying other people's work only in order to better understand how netsuke and other miniature pieces are carved and to master all the necessary techniques. The real joy of carving can only be fully appreciated by producing a finished item from your own original ideas.

Carving netsuke pieces will hopefully give you and many others a great deal of pleasure and satisfaction. You never know, it may change your whole approach to carving. It has mine.

Peter Benson

Russell Birch hard at work carving netsuke in his converted loft

The history of netsuke

Between the sixteenth and nineteenth centuries, wealthy Japanese men would wear the traditional kimono. As this form of dress had no pockets, it was difficult to carry money or other valuables. A purse or pouch therefore had to be tucked into the sash from where it could easily be lost or stolen. This is how the netsuke came about.

Netsuke were designed as a simple device, a form of toggle, attached to the upper end of a silk cord through *himotoshi* (the holes). A cord from which is suspended the *sagemono* (a case for small objects) or *inro* (a case of several individual sections) that contained valuables.

Originally, netsuke would simply have been a small piece of root, twig or even a pebble with holes in. There was no need to use anything of value. In fact, it was not until the Edo period (1615–1868) that the netsuke took on any real significance. At this time, fashion became a supreme measure of taste and status in the cities, with large sums of money being spent on elegant dress and accessories.

Development

It is difficult to find accurate information on how netsuke developed. The details appear to be determined by the person providing the information; consequently, there are as many variations on the origins of this art form as there are types of netsuke. One school of thought casts doubt on whether netsuke were even worn very often, but rather collected as miniature treasures from the very beginning. However, the mythology that has developed around netsuke has a large degree of fact attached to it. The gist of which is as follows:

During the Edo period the borders of Japan were closed to all foreigners, except for the Dutch and the Chinese as their trade played an essential part in the Japanese economy. Although they were allowed into the country, the Dutch and Chinese traders remained under close scrutiny. They also became the subject of incredible curiosity on the part of the Japanese population who, with limited experience of the outside world, perceived these foreigners as being very strange indeed.

Understandably, they were depicted in a wide variety of Japanese art forms, particularly the netsuke, usually in a humorous and sometimes 'tongue-in-cheek' manner. Many of the early netsuke pieces had a vaguely mocking element that has been continued in several contemporary examples. They were also seen as a way of representing folklore, religious and historical figures.

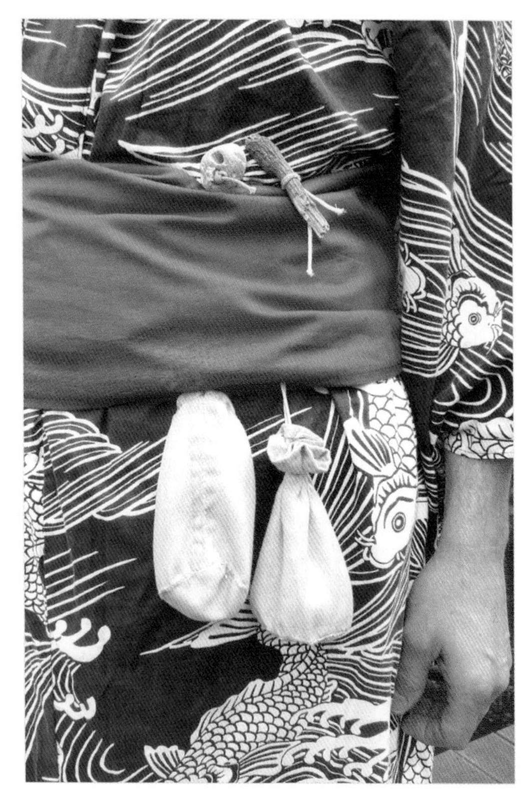
Traditional, functional use of the netsuke

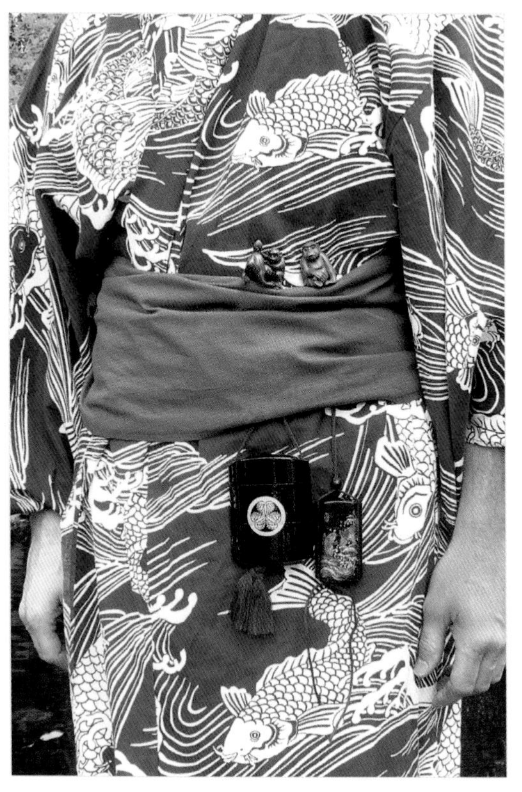
Modern, artistic netsuke and *inro*

This set the tone of netsuke carvings as portraying a rather askance view on life that has continued to modern times. It also set in motion a new art form, which became a major part of collectable sculpture throughout the world.

Once netsuke were accepted as part of the traditional dress, they became an integral part of the culture and history of the Japanese nation. The production of netsuke has continued for centuries, and despite the fact that many current carvers come from outside Japan, the Japanese heritage is never far away from their work.

Netsuke became, and still are, much more than carvings to the carvers, collectors and Japanese people; they are a view on life, a window out onto the world. A true netsuke will always evoke an emotion or reaction, probably more than most other art forms. It is difficult to design and produce such a carving and still remain uninvolved.

Western influence

During the 1850s, Commander Matthew Perry arrived in Japan with an American fleet of ships and once again opened it up to the rest of the world. This led to a decline in Japanese traditional dress in favour of more western styles, as well as the near demise of the use of netsuke. However, westerners were fascinated by these miniature carvings and what they portrayed. The numerous public and private collections that started have continued to grow ever since.

The fact that netsuke were no longer functional items did not appear to detract from their popularity, but it did subtly change their design. Today there is still a need for each one to be recognized as a toggle with the necessary holes to form the *himotoshi*. Where previously size and shape were not seen as critical, now good netsuke need to 'feel right' and also tend to be smaller in size.

Form and materials

Although most people associate netsuke with ivory, this was often too expensive for the carvers and therefore not used as much as was generally thought. Many of the early netsuke were carved in hardwoods like cherry or boxwood.

There are several different types of netsuke available, the earliest being the *manju*, a round solid shape resembling a rice or bean curd cake. Others include the *sashi*, an elongated form of netsuke where the lower part is tucked into the belt of the kimono (*obi*), and the common mask. Yet by far the most popular netsuke is the *katabori*, which is carved on all sides including the underneath.

Traditionally, netsuke are carved in great detail, requiring a vast amount and intricacy of work by the *netsuke-shi's*. This is particularly difficult for the carver as most of the carving is done with the block held in the hand and provision needs to be made for holding it securely. It is this need for almost compulsive detailed work that has contributed to the enormous popularity of netsuke as an art form.

A Japanese carved lacquered wood *inro*

A Japanese ivory and *shibayama* four sectioned *inro*, decorated with bees on hive, with similar *shibayama* netsuke

GETTING STARTED

Planning

With all carving projects, the majority of work takes place before you even pick up your tools. Too many carvers come up with an idea, rush out to find a piece of timber and are hacking lumps off it within minutes. They have no definite ideas about what they are hoping to achieve or the pitfalls that they may encounter.

Producing a pattern before starting to carve is essential. I have never agreed with the opinion that carvers can see what they want in a blank piece of wood and only have to bring it out. Success, to my mind, can only be achieved after considerable planning.

Design

It is important to set simple design constraints for your work. At the top of your list should be ensuring that the netsuke feels good with no unappealing projections or sharp edges.

Contemporary designs should be carved in simple shapes, usually a sphere or an ovoid. Restricting your early designs to these shapes will help to avoid undue heartache and will make it easier to focus on the design parameters. Either start with a shape, and fit your subject(s) into it, or choose a subject and make the shape fit. Either way works equally well, and indeed most carvers use both in their work. As your confidence increases, you can become much more adventurous.

Once you have chosen your subject and shape, experiment with your designs using modelling clay or plasticine. I recommend making a maquette for each netsuke, as they are ideal for visualizing and testing shapes and ideas (see page 18). Interestingly, I have found that many carvers will pick up and play with a small piece of plasticine or clay to experiment with various designs when the piece is a miniature netsuke, but are reluctant to do so when the carving is any bigger.

Character

There are several different types of netsuke, each with its own requirements and attraction for the carver. Each netsuke should have a character of its own, which may include a message or a story. Often humorous and hidden surprise areas can add to its attraction. Ultimately, carving netsuke offers carvers a chance to show off their skills, they should therefore be exquisite.

Most of the pieces in this book come under the heading of *katabori*, which means 'carved all round', without any base or backing. As the pieces are carved underneath, as well as on top, they need to be picked up and handled to really appreciate the craftsmanship. It is therefore a pity that there is a need to display them behind glass to protect them from theft.

The leaf has been used to avoid carving the rabbit's feet

An advanced netsuke with several areas that could easily break off

One problem with this style is in reference to carving animals. You need to know what the bottom of their feet look like in order to carve the animal accurately. This can be difficult as there is limited reference material available. The alternative is to sit the animal on a leaf, a log, or something similar to hide the soles of their feet; see for example the rabbit on a cabbage leaf, shown above.

On the plus side, capturing the essence or 'jizz' of the animal is more important than anatomical accuracy. The viewer should be able to recognize what the subject is even if it has not got the correct number of fingers or its fur is not quite right. Therefore, your research should focus on the animal's behaviour rather than its appearance, although an understanding of both is important.

Even when you have chosen your subject, done the research and got all the tools together, you still need to make some contingency plans to cover any potential problems.

Look at your design to see whether there are any parts that may break off during the carving process and therefore need to be supported or modified. You can also leave extra wood in potential problem areas, so that you can make minor changes if things do go wrong (see page 37).

Although the carving of the fox above epitomises the character of the netsuke, there are some very vulnerable areas that could very easily be damaged. I would certainly not recommend this to a novice carver – too much can go wrong. It is important to make sure that you can actually carve what you have designed and that you have the necessary tools for the job.

The piece shown below left, on the other hand, is considered 'safe'. There are no vulnerable areas and the whole piece feels right.

The sheep pictured below right shows how the carver has supported the feet in the design to keep them secure.

This carving of guinea pigs is unlikely to be broken during the carving process

Here the feet have been carved purposely to prevent them from being damaged

Maquettes and patterns

Maquette is the French word for 'scale model' and usually refers to a small three-dimensional model or study of an intended work. The main reason for constructing a model prior to carving is to solve any design issues. After all, it is much easier to play around with clay or plasticine than to experiment when carving. It also gives you the opportunity to explore your design from every angle.

People make maquettes using a wide variety of materials. I tend to use either plasticine or modelling clay, depending on the size of the piece. Occasionally I will experiment with soft wood, such as basswood or jelutong, to see whether an idea is practical. Surprisingly, not every idea or design is possible or practical in the chosen material and is better rejected at this stage. Modelling wax can also be effective, particularly if you are working with very small pieces.

Dormouse maquette (in plasticine)

Making maquettes

I recommend making a fairly rudimentary working maquette just to get started; this can be developed alongside the carving. If you encounter a problem, you can immediately go back to the maquette to solve it before returning to the carving. It is never a good idea to experiment with your carving or to carve without a firm idea of what you are doing.

Many carvers, however, make their maquettes as detailed as possible, measuring each part accurately before starting the carving process. Although this is an effective method for professional carvers who have to recreate an accepted design, it can make for a rather stressful journey for the enthusiastic hobby carver.

Copying models is very difficult and also tends to eliminate any kind of spontaneity from the carving. In my opinion, carvers should be free to go where the mood, design and materials lead them within the limits they set themselves.

Collect anything you find that is even tentatively associated with the subject. Scour bookshops, the Internet, magazines, or any other source that may be of use. Once you think you have collected enough material, start to make your maquette. Work out the basic shape you require, before creating it out of clay or plasticine. Do not restrict yourself by the size, just let it happen naturally. You can make life very hard for yourself if you are constantly checking the dimensions. At this stage, it is also important to check that your tools can get into those awkward little areas.

If you are repeating a previous carving, then use the original as the maquette; this will provide you with most of the information that you will need.

Making patterns

Once you have made your maquette, transfer the information to your block ready to start carving. This should not be too difficult. Simply hold your maquette over a piece of plain paper and draw round the outline. You might need just one outline or one from every side – remember to make a note of which side you have drawn.

When you have decided on the size of your carving, reduce the outline from your maquette to the same size – most computer printers will do this for you. Check and double check that the patterns are the same scale, are on the correct sides and are also the right way round – you would be surprised how many carvers get this wrong.

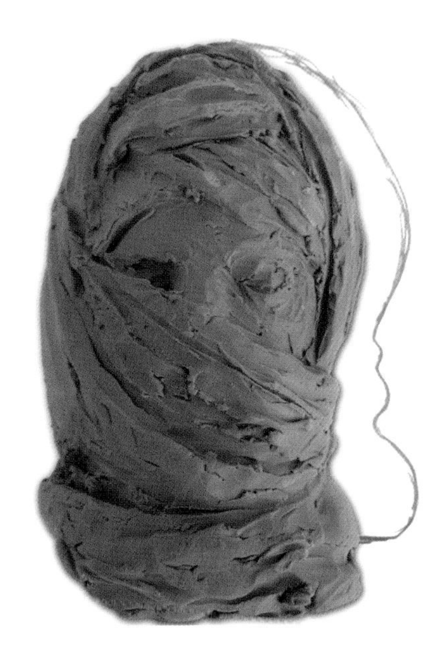

Pattern for the mask taken from the maquette

The pattern

1 Transfer your pattern from the maquette onto your material. This can be done either by sticking the paper directly onto the material or by drawing round it with a white pencil.

2 Next, cut around the outline using a bandsaw or a coping saw.

3 This should leave you with a block of material which is the same shape as your pattern.

Materials

Netsuke can be carved from almost any available material. There are many fine examples in wood, ivory, ceramics, tagua nut, buffalo horn, amber and even stone. Netsuke carvers delight in using all kinds of materials, many of which other carvers would dismiss out of hand.

I would suggest starting to carve with wood and sticking with it until you have quite a bit of experience in carving very small pieces. Not only is it easier to work with, in my opinion it is also much more pleasurable.

Wood

Although you can use almost any wood to carve netsuke, some species are more suitable than others. In general, you need wood with a very close grain that will take fine detail. This applies to many home-grown species, as well as several exotics. Your choice will therefore depend on how easy it is to obtain a particular timber and the amount of fine detail that is required for the particular design you have chosen. The less detail required, the wider the choice of timber available to you. Generally, the harder the wood the finer the detail you are able to carve.

Boxwood, which is a particular favourite of mine, is probably the most suitable wood to use for netsuke. Although I prefer the home-grown variety, I have also been very happy with both castello and Brazilian boxwood. As long as you avoid the small logs, as these could contain tiny cracks in the centre, you should have no problems. If you find these difficult to get hold of boxwood, lemonwood is very similar, easier to source and a pleasure to carve.

The more common fruitwoods like apple, pear, plum and cherry should not be overlooked. They all carve very well indeed and hold very fine detail. You may even like to try them 'green' or undried, as they are generally much softer.

Working with undried timber

Using undried or 'green' timber for carving is not a problem, as long as you liberally oil the end grain whenever you stop carving for any length of time as it is here that the most moisture is lost. Also, do not subject the carving to significant changes of temperature as this will disrupt the drying process and cracks may occur.

If you prefer to carve exotic woods, only use ones that have an obvious fine grain. Bear in mind that exotic species often have a stronger grain pattern that may not be appropriate for your chosen design. For something softer, a good piece of lime will give you a very good finish with fine detail. It requires a lot more time and effort to achieve this finish, but it is easier to carve.

Boxwood is the most common timber used to carve netsuke

Lime will provide a very good finish with fine detail

Ivory

Netsuke carvers tend to be very curious when it comes to what materials they can use, and will try almost anything. If it works they use it, if not it is rejected.

Although most people associate netsuke with ivory, this was often too expensive for carvers in the past. While it remains popular, with the high degree of sensitivity and various legal limitations, ivory is not seen as a commercial proposition. However, as long as it is purchased legally, ivory can still be used by professional carvers to create pieces for their personal collections.

Many carvers now source ivory from pre-1925 snooker or billiard balls found in sales or in charity shops. These balls can be obtained relatively cheaply and are ideal for netsuke carving. There is no need to obtain a certificate, as they are antique pieces. Having said this, you will still find it difficult to sell your work, as you cannot prove the source of the ivory.

If you wish to buy ivory in tusk form, ensure that you check the legal implications and also find a legitimate ivory merchant from whom you can get licenced ivory. It is also possible to purchase legal mammoth ivory, although it tends to be very expensive.

Be on your guard though, there are many unscrupulous people out there who will try to sell you substitute ivory. There are several tales of unsuspecting collectors paying large sums of money for ivory netsuke that was in fact plastic.

To check whether the netsuke is genuine ivory, heat a needle or nail to red hot, then place it on the piece. If the ivory is genuine, the needle will not leave a mark. Most respectable ivory salesmen will have the necessary equipment to do this, as it is a recognized test.

Tagua nut

Alternatively, if you want the netsuke to look like ivory without actually using the real thing, you might like to try using tagua nuts. When finished and polished, the appearance of these nuts is remarkably like that of ivory. They do, however, have a void in the middle, so there are limits to the kind of designs that you can carve and there is also an increased need for flexibility.

Horn, antler and amber

Other materials you might like to carve with include buffalo horn, which is mostly black or dark brown, and ram's horn, which is much lighter, ranging from almost translucent to a rich tan colour. Both of these materials can be carved with chisels or knives, although much quicker results can be achieved with rotary burrs. When working with these materials it is very important to wear a mask and a pair of goggles, as well as using some form of dust extraction (see page 34). Buffalo horn and ram's horn are particularly superb materials, together with deer antler and amber, for making eyes (see page 43).

Miscellaneous

Netsuke carvers delight in using all sorts of interesting bits and pieces, which most other carvers would not even think of using. Lots of fun can be had finding unusual things to include in your work.

Netsuke carvers collect *umimatsu* (fossilized coral), rocks, twigs, sea shells, attractive pieces of coral, horn and so on. Anything that can be used is regarded as precious and is stored carefully away until it is needed. This is one of the more interesting aspects of research and can lead to unique pieces of work. Never underestimate the value of searching for and collecting materials; the results are what make carvings special.

Finishes

If you already carve, you will probably have a range of different finishes in your workshop, including one that you prefer.

As netsuke have to be handled to be truly appreciated, I am not keen on finishing them with any sort of wax as this can become dirty very easily, spoiling the look and feel of the piece.

I prefer to use oil, of which there are many options. Applying several coats to your carving provides a really attractive shine. The advantage of using oil is that the netsuke can be washed clean should it get dirty from handling. If it loses its shine, further coats can be applied. The only thing I will add is that every product has its own characteristics, so you should carefully read and follow the instructions provided in order to get the best results.

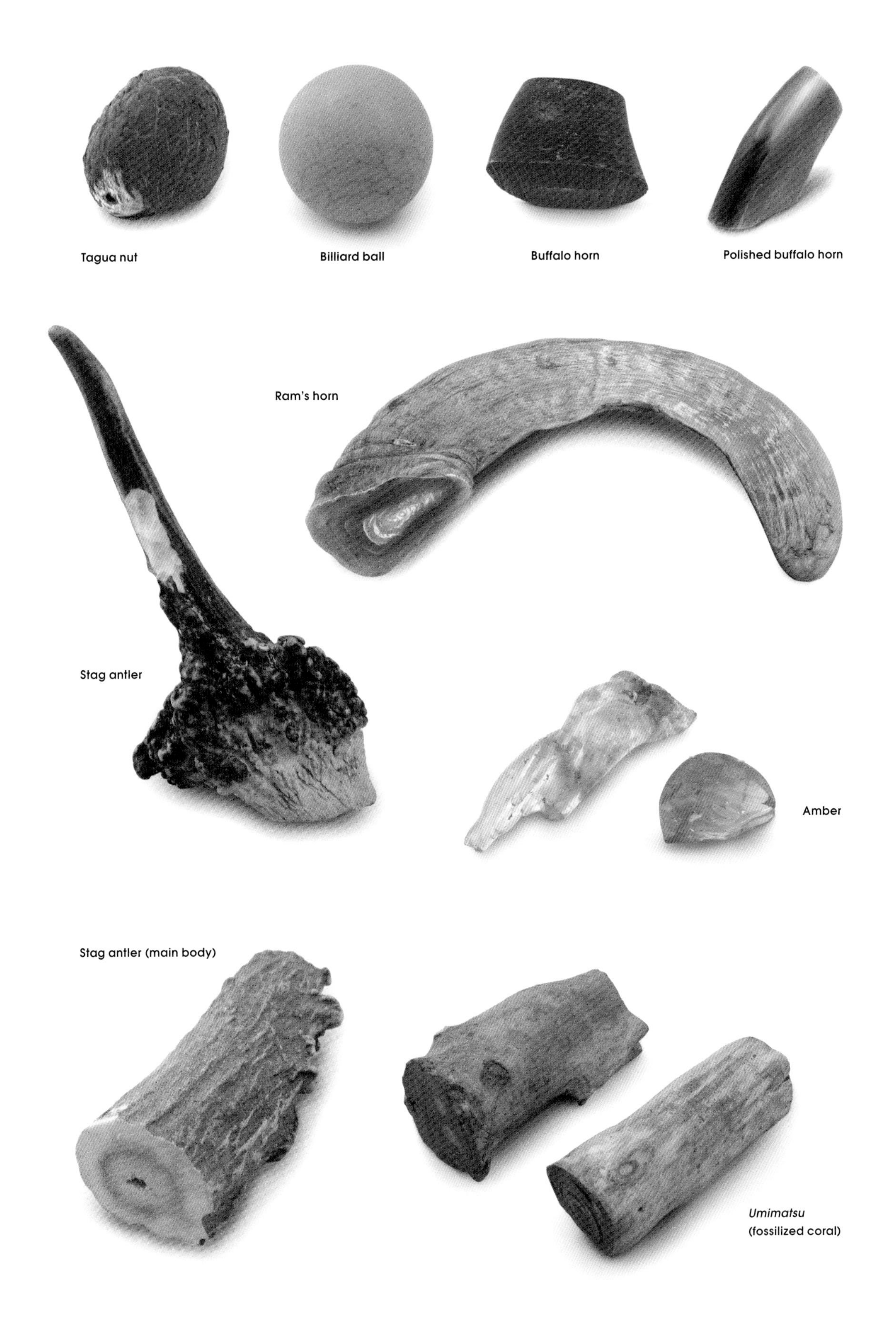
Tagua nut

Billiard ball

Buffalo horn

Polished buffalo horn

Ram's horn

Stag antler

Amber

Stag antler (main body)

Umimatsu (fossilized coral)

Tools and equipment

Most tool manufacturers will stock an extensive range of tools suitable for completing the majority of the work required. However, only a few will make tools that are small enough to create the finer details.

Hand tools

You will need standard-sized tools to do the initial roughing out, as it is hard work trying to hold the block of wood in your hand while at the same time trying to remove most of the waste. Holding your work in a vice makes this job much easier.

Next, you will need several small hand tools, commonly referred to as palm gouges or blockcutters. There is a large choice available, with companies producing many different designs. Personally, I prefer to purchase mine from companies that supply tools directly from the factory, as they can often make tools to my own design.

The list below covers the tools you need to complete all the projects in this book. Having said this, you can use any tools you already have if you prefer, as long as they do the job.

Basic toolbox

Palm tools or block cutters

1 $\frac{1}{8}$in (3mm) number 1 or 2 chisel
2 $\frac{1}{8}$in (3mm) number 3 gouge
3 $\frac{1}{16}$in (1.5mm) number 39 V tool
4 $\frac{1}{4}$in (6mm) number 3 gouge
5 $\frac{1}{4}$in (6mm) number 9 gouge
6 $\frac{1}{16}$in (1.5mm) number 9 or 11 veiner
7 $\frac{3}{16}$in (4.5mm) number 2 skew chisel
8 $\frac{3}{16}$in (4.5mm) number 9 gouge

9 A small but heavy mallet is an invaluable tool for roughing out.

Full-sized gouge

10 $\frac{1}{4}$in (6mm) number 3 gouge (fish-tail or straight)
11 $\frac{1}{4}$in (6mm) number 9 gouge (fish-tail or straight)

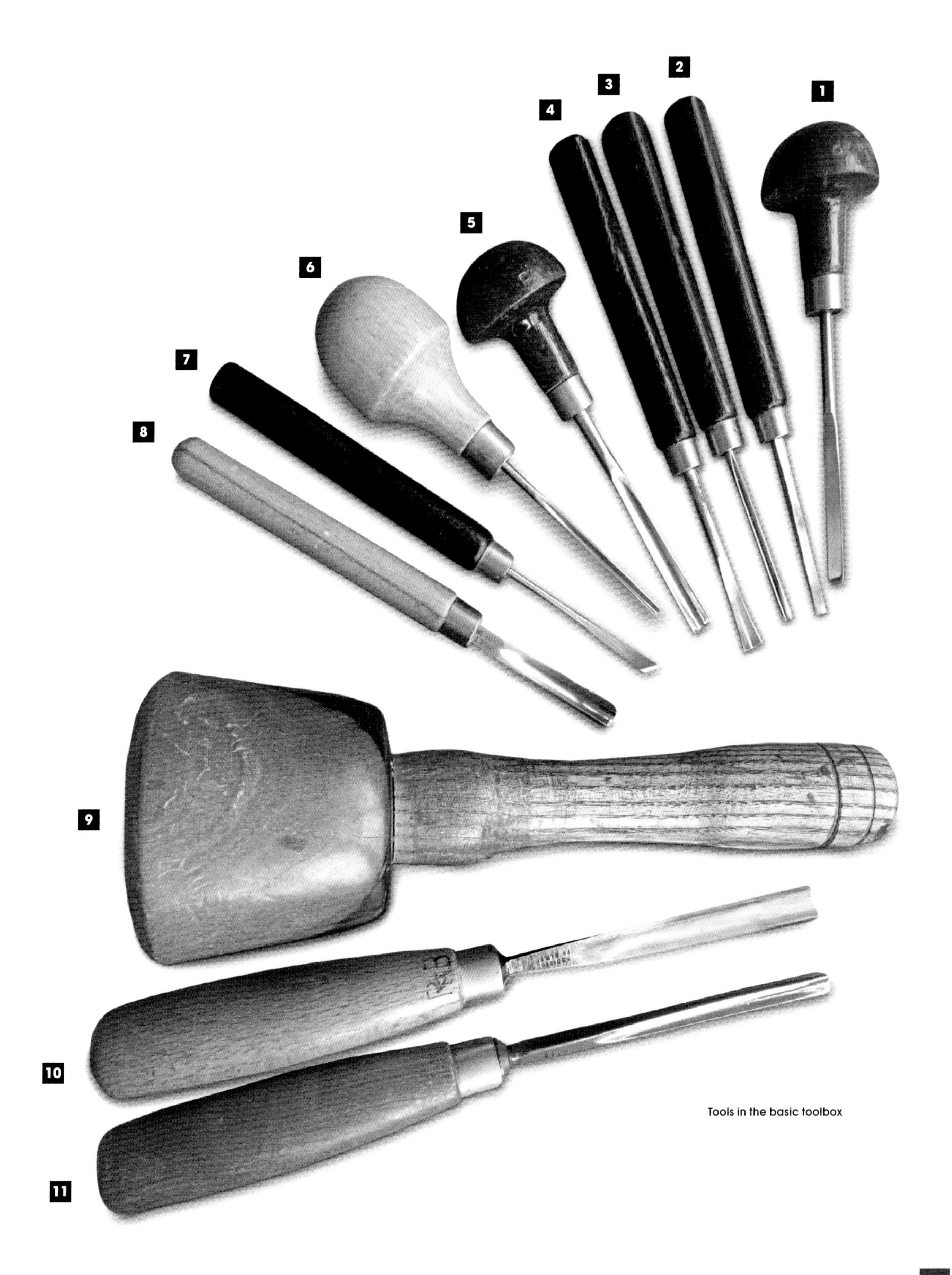

Tools in the basic toolbox

Narrower handles are designed to be held like a pen and are better for fine detail

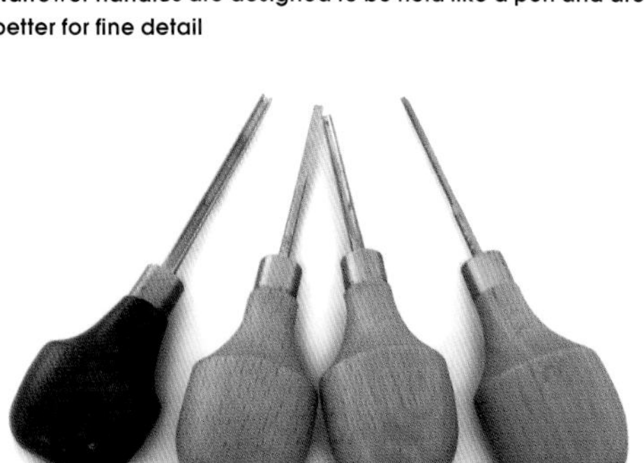

Wider-shaped handles can be easier to hold

Options

I often use different-shaped handles. You might also like to change the handles or even choose different tools from those in the basic toolbox on page 24. Compare the two sorts of palm tools above, which incorporate different handles.

For the very fine details you will need to use special tools. You might like to take a look at the Dockyard range (see page 158 for suppliers) to start with as they make a variety of tiny chisels and gouges.

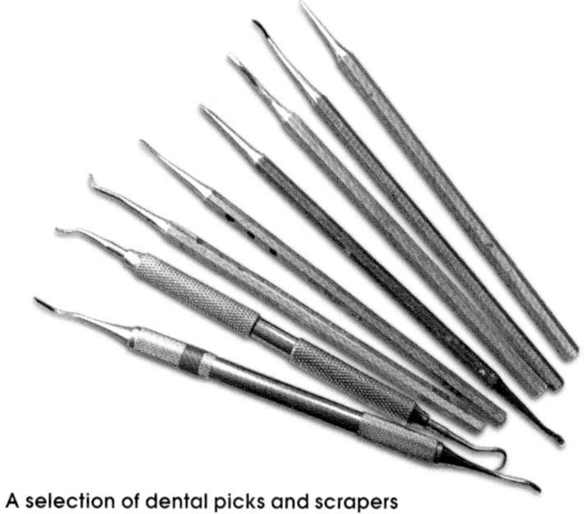

A selection of dental picks and scrapers

If you need to go smaller still, you will need to make or modify the tools yourself. For example, I have discovered that picks used in dental practices are a great alternative for a very fine chisel when carving fine details.

When you move on to using other materials or undertaking more complicated designs, you will almost certainly need a selection of very small scrapers for those difficult-to-reach nooks and crannies. You will need to make these yourself as they become necessary. Further information on creating your own can be found on page 30.

TIP: **To avoid the risk of cutting your hand while carving small pieces, try holding the tool like a pen. Keep your third and fourth fingers in contact with the wood and your two thumbs in contact with each other.**

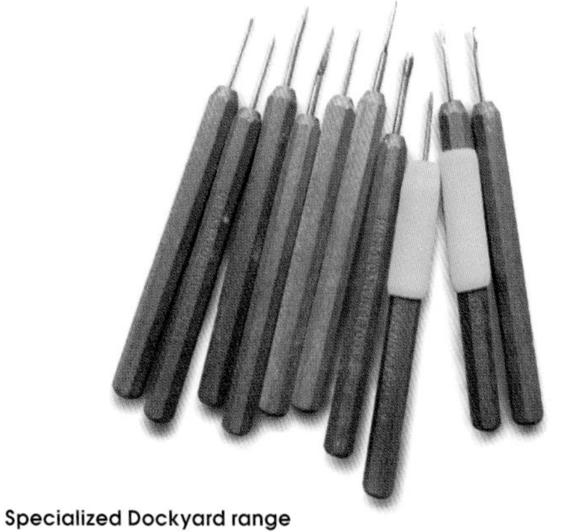

Specialized Dockyard range

A homemade or modified selection of tools

Lighting and magnifiers

You will certainly benefit from a good light when you are carving small details, and also some kind of magnifier if you are working for any length of time. Some of the best-known magnifying visors contain a series of magnifying lenses fitted into a head unit and can be purchased with or without lights fitted to either side. However, there are many cheaper versions available which do a similar job, such as the one shown in the picture below. There is also a range of magnifying lenses on stands that you may prefer, details of which can be found in magazines and tool catalogues.

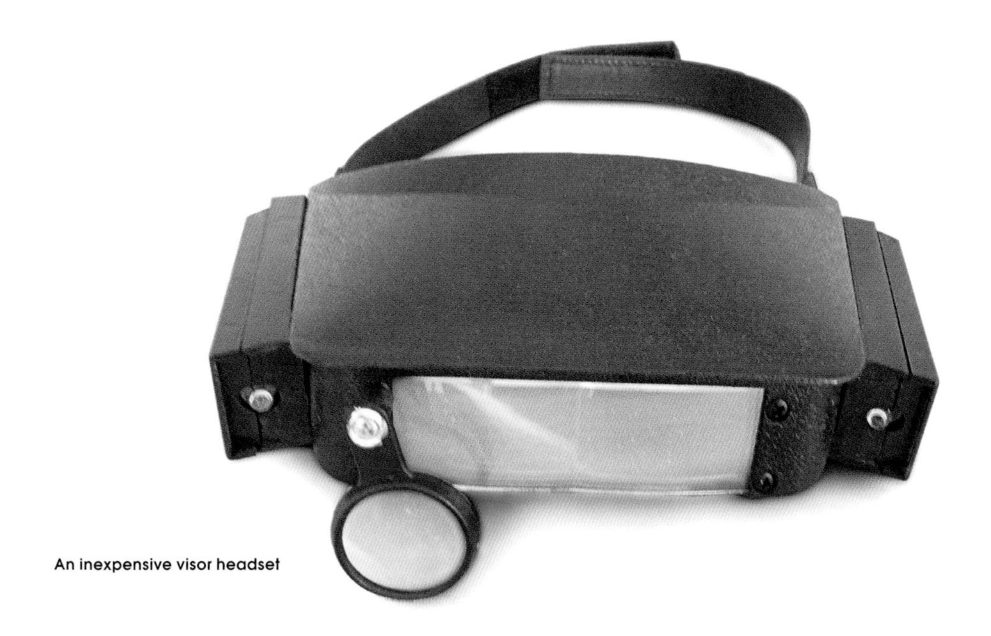

An inexpensive visor headset

Holding devices

There is little need for expensive clamps, vices or other holding devices. If you are using hand tools, a small, cheap vice or carving post is all that you should need. You can easily make the post yourself, and a suitable vice can be purchased from a range of DIY stores at very little cost.

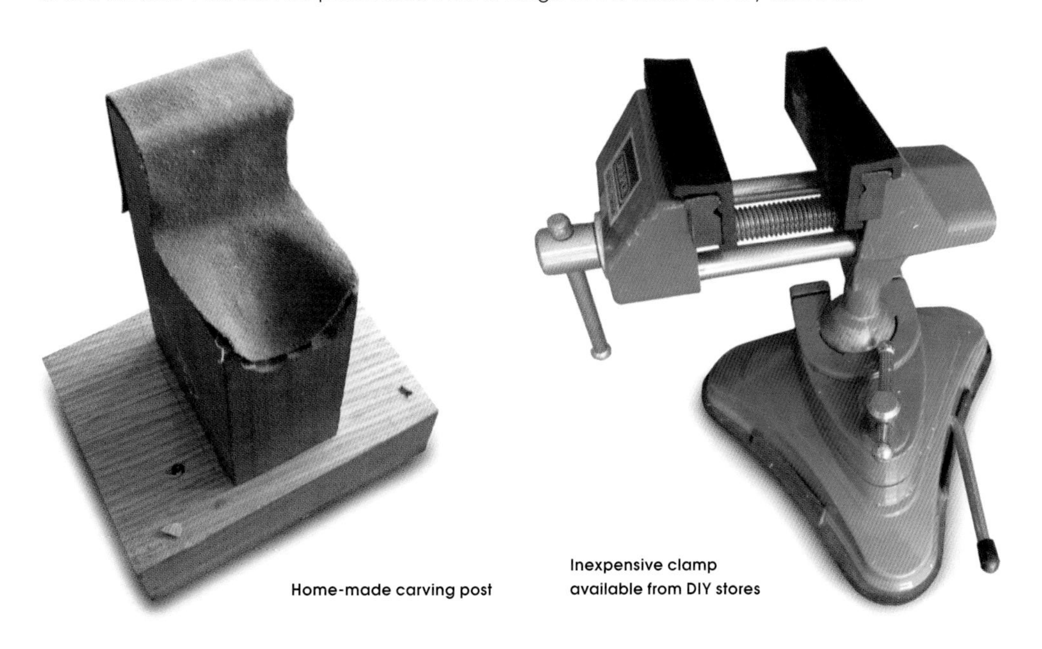

Home-made carving post

Inexpensive clamp available from DIY stores

Abrasives

Any abrasives that are suitable for wood can be used on miniature carvings. However, it is important to ensure that you only use the fine grits. Anything too coarse can leave deep scratch marks that are difficult to remove on something as small as a netsuke.

The range of grits you are likely to need run from around 120 grit through to 600. These abrasives will suffice for the initial smoothing, providing a smooth surface with minimal scratching, but unfortunately they are not fine enough for the final finish.

To achieve a good finish on something this small you will have to spend quite a lot of time sanding and smoothing the surface. Even the smallest of imperfections in the finish will spoil the overall effect. Abrasives that go much finer, down to 12,000 grit, are ideal for providing a good finishing shine, even when you are working with ivory or horn.

Cloth-backed abrasives are preferable and are available up to 12,000 grit. They can be obtained from specialist suppliers (see page 158 for details). These are not only more effective than the paper-backed variety, but they are far easier to use and last much longer. Even better, in my opinion, are the cellular abrasives that can easily be cleared of any clogging material and can also be washed.

When using materials other than wood, you could also try abrasives such as scouring pads, metal polish, pumice or polishing compounds. When using horn, tagua or ivory, you might like to try razor strop fungus. This is commonly found on old silver birch trees and, once sliced and dried, will polish to a high finish at no cost at all.

If you are using power tools, a browse through any tool catalogue will bring to light a whole range of abrasives that can be fitted to your motor. I suggest getting hold of a selection and deciding for yourself which suits your requirements.

The main difficulty with any finishing of miniature pieces is accessibility. You can overcome this by purchasing or making sanding sticks of many different shapes to get into all those awkward little corners. Odd-shaped bits of wood with pieces of abrasive fixed firmly to the end are a great help. Many carving problems can be solved with a little ingenuity.

Very fine grit abrasives

Cloth-backed abrasives

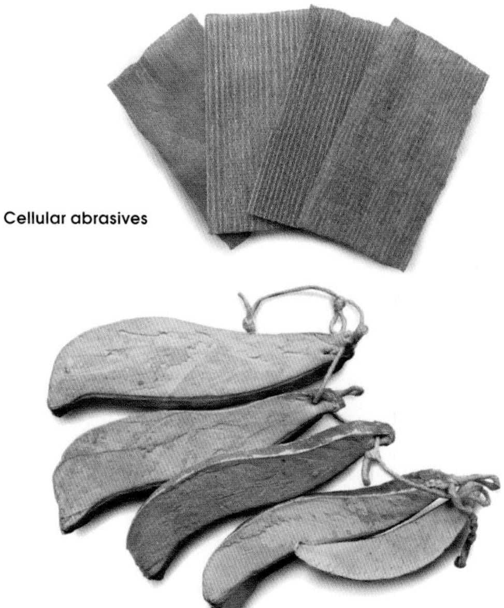

Cellular abrasives

Razor strop fungus cut and strung to dry

Power tools

As I get older, I find it increasingly difficult to hold a tool in my fingers and to carve for anything like as long as I used to, especially when using hard woods or other materials. I have therefore resigned myself to joining the power carvers with their noise, vibration and dust, at least for part of the time.

There is a wide choice of machines available to suit all budgets. As with most things, you get what you pay for. I would suggest that you purchase something relatively inexpensive until you are certain that you want to go down the power-carving route with all that it entails.

Whichever one you choose, check that it is suitable for lateral pressure – this means that the cutter or burr is used with the side doing the cutting rather than the end. Many of the least expensive machines specifically state that they are only suitable for drilling. These machines tend to run much slower than the more expensive micromotor machines. Although they are good machines with which to start carving, they tend to be much noisier and vibrate more. This is something to consider, particularly if you intend to work in the house.

Alternatively, micromotor machines are significantly more expensive, but quieter and pretty much vibration-free.

A typical budget system

You need to bear in mind that these small machines only take small shank cutters. If you want to use one on bigger work, as well as with heavy-duty cutters, you could go for a suspended carving unit.

Whatever your preference or your budget, I recommend taking the time to have a good look round at what is available before making your choice.

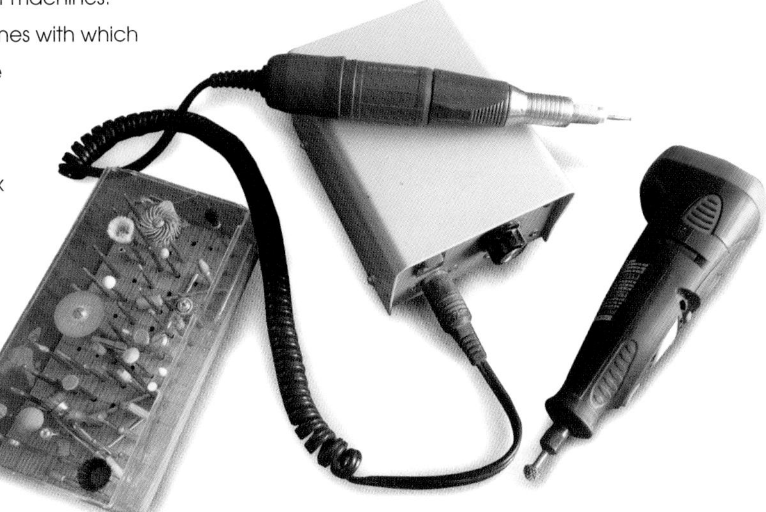

A micromoter (centre) and rechargeable machine with accessories

Making and modifying tools

When you start carving miniature pieces you embark on a completely new aspect of carving. Gone are the generalizations about tools, sharpening, grain direction and so on. Everything you produce will be small enough to fit into a generously sized egg cup and will, therefore, require specially adapted tools.

You cannot simply go down to your local tool supplier and kit yourself out with everything you need. Instead, you are more likely to become quite an expert at modifying left-over bits of metal into wonderful specialist tools and adapting odds and ends to reach particularly awkward corners.

Dental picks

The tools that you are most likely to need are a selection of dental picks. The picks come in an astounding range of shapes and sizes. They are ideal for reaching difficult places and can also be ground into chisels of varying widths. They can usually be obtained from your dentist or from dental equipment suppliers. Avoid those found at tool sales as the steel they are made from is insufficient for holding an edge suitable for carving.

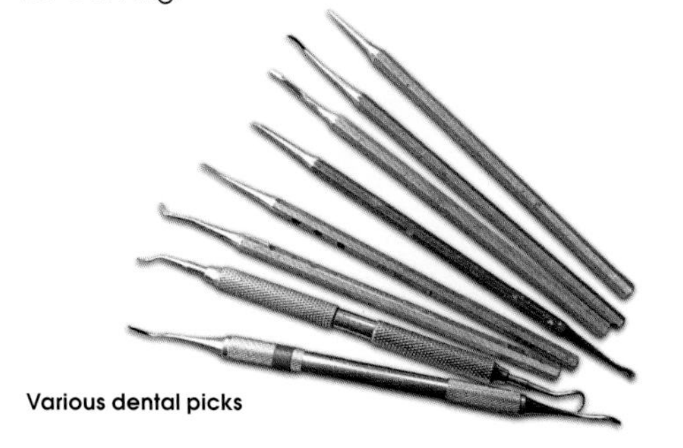

Various dental picks

TIP: If you are using a bench grinder to shape your tools, do not let the steel overheat as this will destroy the tool's temper. As a guide, the tool should never get too hot to hold in your hand. If in doubt, cut the end off at the required length, then sharpen the edge on an oil stone and finally hone it on leather.

Old files

These files are ideal for making into small tools. Soften the steel by heating it until it is red hot, then let it cool down slowly. Hammer or shape the tool to whatever shape is required, grinding it to refine the shape as many times as necessary, and file the tool. When you are satisfied, heat the tool again in the same way, before quenching it in water or oil to harden it. Although the tool will now be hard, it will also be very brittle and could therefore break in use. There are several ways to temper the tool, but by far the easiest method is to pop it into an oven heated to 350°F (176°C) for around two hours, before leaving it to cool thoroughly. Finally, give the tool a suitable handle and you are ready to go.

Masonry nails

My favourite source of steel for small tools is masonry nails. These are both readily available and inexpensive. They are also around the right size, so there is no need to cut the steel. The process of transforming these nails into useable tools differs slightly, yet it is much more straightforward than other methods.

Soften the nail as before. This might take a bit longer and you may need to get the nail hotter than cherry red. Let it cool slowly, then shape it to whatever you require by grinding and filing the nail. When you have the right shape, harden and quench the tool, as described earlier. Do not temper it afterwards or it will not hold its edge in use.

1 Soften the nail over a heat source.

2 Hammer it into the shape required.

3 Grind the nail into shape.

4 Further grinding may be required.

5 To finish, file the nail.

6 It is now ready for hardening.

TIP: **If you need to make larger tools, or even a wider variety, there are several tool companies that can provide you with suitable tool steel and advice on how to achieve the best results. It is always worth asking for this advice as it is generally very useful.**

Chisels

Most of the smaller tools you will need will be chisels. Making or modifying these is pretty simple. Producing gouges or V tools, on the other hand, can be slightly more complicated. A rotary power tool kit will have some small grinding bits or cutting wheels suitable for shaping these tools.

Scrapers

Obviously, if you are going to work with materials other than wood the tools you require will be very diverse. Different-shaped scrapers will probably be most useful. These can be made in the same way as small chisels, except that the ends need to be shaped to suit a scraping action instead of a cutting one. Again, I suggest that you form these to match your requirements rather than make them beforehand. Producing tools 'just in case' can often be a time-wasting exercise. You will soon build up a collection of the most popular shapes.

A selection of different-shaped scrapers

SAFETY WARNING: **If you are using blowlamps, make sure you are working in a safe environment away from flammable material and, ideally, wear heat-resistant gloves. With this process and any power grinding or cutting you should always wear safety glasses** **(see pages 34–36).**

Maintaining your tools

There are several ways to produce a bevel on conventional carving tools including oilstones, diamond or ceramic blocks, or one of the many power systems. Unfortunately, many of these are difficult to use with the very small tools used to carve netsuke, so experimentation is necessary.

There are two parts to keeping any gouge or chisel sharp – producing a suitable bevel, then maintaining (or honing) the edge. Scrapers and knives need to be kept sharp using a stone of some kind and possibly a leather strop. Some of the smaller gouges and chisels can also be sharpened this way, although, unless you wear a magnifier, the edge can be very difficult to see. This is particularly the case with very small V tools, which can be easily ruined by poor sharpening.

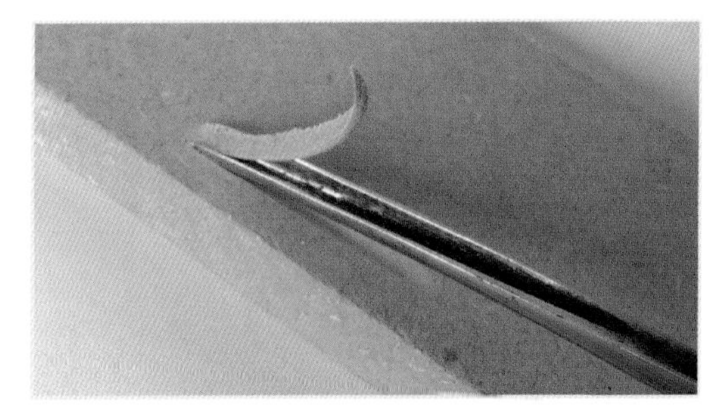

First cut

One method I have found to keep these small tools successfully honed is to use a block of MDF. Offcuts of MDF can be obtained for next to nothing. To hone gouges and V tools, simply cut a groove in the surface with each tool, then drag it back along this groove. The profile of the tool is maintained and the edge remains sharp.

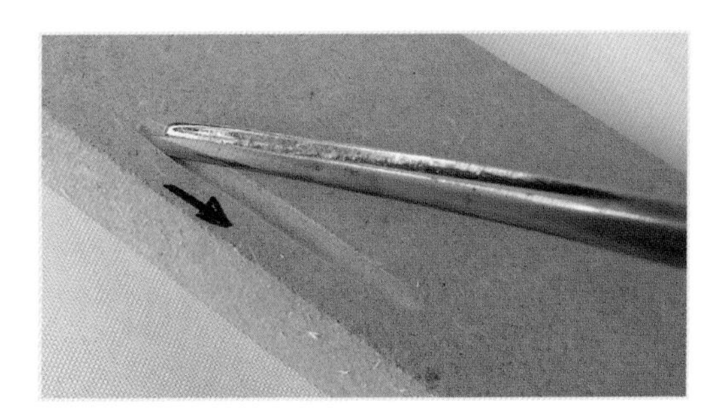

Drag tool

The secret to any successful sharpening is to do it frequently – about every 30 minutes or so. What you are really looking to do is just to hone the tool and not let it get blunt enough to need grinding. MDF is very abrasive and, in general, should not need any honing compound. It will glaze after a while and, when it does, add some compound or simply cut another groove.

The important things to bear in mind are, firstly, to keep the bevel of the tool flat, particularly close to the cutting edge, and secondly to make sure that there are no nicks or burrs at this edge. With continuous use the bevel will tend to round off and will then need flattening on a stone or on another abrasive surface.

Safety

It is essential to follow safe working practices at all times. This is easy to appreciate when you are working with large, powerful machines, yet even when you are carving miniature netsuke pieces there are some very serious risks to consider.

You can still do a lot of harm; for instance, inhaling dust or accidently sticking a sharp tool into your hand. Believe me, I have the scars to prove it, mostly inflicted during the short periods when I forgot to put my glove on or when I lost my concentration.

When embarking on any project, the carver must be aware of the safety factors that apply: correct holding devices, good lighting, sharp tools, a good working surface and any of the necessary protective equipment or clothing.

Gloves

The carver will invariably hold the carving in one of their hands for some of the time, and most cuts will be made towards the holding hand. While there is quite a lot of resistance to wearing protective gloves, I advise anyone new to carving miniature pieces to purchase a good pair of gloves with high ratings on blade cut and puncture resistance, or at the very least one for the non-carving hand.

These gloves will not provide a great deal of protection against a stabbing cut, but they will definitely reduce the damage done by a slashing cut and should always be worn when working with a knife. Having said that, unless specifically recommended, this type of glove should not be worn when using power tools, particularly those with rotary burrs. These can catch the fabric and inflict serious damage to any parts of the body that are close by.

As you gain experience in carving, you will devise protective strategies with regard to how you hold the tool and the carving material. At this later stage, you will probably prefer to work without a glove – it certainly makes for a much more comfortable and precise grip.

A selection of gloves for protection

Carving post

Another option is to use a small carving post on a board or to work on an old table top. That said, holding the block firmly can be difficult when you are working with miniature pieces. When carving with wood, always allow for an extra length of timber under the block, so that you can hold it firmly. This is not as easy when you are using other materials like ivory or buffalo horn. If, like me, you only carve ivory from old billiard or snooker balls, there is nothing other than the ball to hold on to. You can always fix this to a small wooden block using a high-strength adhesive.

Magnifier equipment for detailed work

Leather apron

If you intend on working with the carving held in your lap, I would heartily recommend purchasing a leather apron, especially for use with power tools. You can do yourself a lot of damage with an out-of-control rotary burr.

Scalpels

The blades in scalpels are brittle and can therefore break easily, sending pieces shooting off in all directions. Ensure you do not work too close to other people and always wear suitable eye protection.

Daylight lamp

Carving netsuke and other miniature pieces can often strain the eyes and lead to long-term problems with your sight. Even if you can see the work clearly, after a long session in poor light you may well end up with double vision. It is also very difficult to see fine detail in poorly lit conditions. Even in a well-lit workshop, I would recommend having a good daylight lamp by your side.

Magnifier

A magnifier is also important in order to protect your eyes. I worked for years with no form of magnification, yet when I finally gave in and used a magnifying visor to complete the fur on the rabbit netsuke, I realized that I had been struggling unnecessarily for all that time. It is incredible how much more you can see with the correct magnifying equipment. Bear in mind that different types suit different people.

Masks and goggles

When carving using power tools make sure you are wearing either a mask or a respirator, as well as protective goggles. Dust and small wood chippings can be very dangerous to your health, especially when they get into your lungs or your eyes. For example, a high proportion of hardwoods produce toxic dust when sanded, which, when inhaled, can cause severe damage to your lungs. You need to be extra careful when carving ivory or buffalo horn, as apart from the dust being an irritant, there is a remote possibility of the material containing anthrax.

Masks and respirator

First aid box

It is important for every carver to have a first aid box close to hand. No matter how careful you are in the workshop, you will inevitably cut yourself at some point. A good supply of plasters and absorbent pads is therefore the minimum you should have.

Applying lotions and potions to a cut is not recommended; a simple plaster will usually suffice. Even with more severe cuts, simply dress the wound with a pad and seek professional help. Do not take any chances. If somebody else cuts themselves, do not be tempted to put anything on the wound except a sterile pad. Many people are violently allergic to elastic plasters and various medication. If they decide that the cut needs a dressing, they should apply it themselves.

Dust extraction unit

If you find yourself particularly taken with netsuke carving or working with ivory or horn, you should install a portable dust extraction unit as an added precaution. Even if you wear a mask, it is of little use if the atmosphere around you is filled with dust particles, which you inhale as soon as you remove the mask. There are small units available for the workshop, or you can make a perfectly serviceable unit yourself at very little cost.

Means of communication

If you frequently work on your own in the workshop, it is also important that you have some sort of communication device to hand, an intercom or mobile phone for example, so that you can get help in an emergency.

SAFETY WARNING: Something that often gets overlooked in workshops is the clearing of any sawdust or shavings. These add to the airborne dust and are also a potential fire risk. I have had two fires in my workshop, one of which was caused by sawdust left on the floor. I had been called away to the phone for just a minute or two, yet by the time I returned all that was left was a line of black ash in front of a scorched bench.

Avoiding and rectifying mistakes

Most problems that occur result from mistakes the carver has made or things they have omitted to do. This may be due to insufficient or incomplete research; a badly thought-out design; or selecting the wrong tools or timber. Mistakes frequently happen, but there are ways to avoid them.

The first step is to plan your project as thoroughly as possible. Collect as much information as you can, scouring the Internet, books, magazines and so on to find anything that may be of use.

Before you start, check that you have the right tools for the job and that you can reach all the awkward areas. Also, search for the best materials. For example, do not settle for cheap offcuts of timber when, for only a small amount more, you can obtain the ideal piece.

While carving, try to anticipate potential problem areas and build in escape routes – extra wood for difficult spots and definitely no undercuts or holes until the end. The ability to sort out unexpected problems confidently separates the novice from the experienced carver. Almost any problem can be put right; how effectively will depend on experience, skill and the amount of time you spend on the carving.

Also ensure that you choose the grain direction carefully to avoid weak areas of short grain. If you do find cavities or faults in the material, you can make up fillers using glue mixed with dust using the same material, although check the colour before using it.

Anything that is very delicate or contains short-grain wood should remain supported for as long as possible. Do not separate these areas from the rest of the carving until the last possible moment. They can also be strengthened by being treated with high-strength adhesive before carving. Birds' beaks and insects' legs, for example, have been carved very successfully with this treatment.

There are often instances where it is simply not possible to repair the damage. Your only option is to modify the design. Invariably, when I have been forced to change my original ideas, the results have been much better than the original. Pieces can be grafted onto carvings, joins can be hidden in creases and folds, hands can be fitted into sleeves and heads can be inserted into collars. Avoid using glue for repairs, except in exceptional circumstances.

Finally, do not work when you are tired or unsure about the next step, as this is when most mistakes occur.

TECHNIQUES

Eyes

Study the eyes of your subject carefully, collecting as many pictures as possible to help you to carve them accurately. Different animals have different eyes, but the basic shape remains the same. Animals of prey have bulging eyes situated on the side of the head, so that they can see behind them. Predators' eyes, on the other hand, face forwards so that they can focus on their prey. Most predators also have prominent brows over their eyes to protect them against impact.

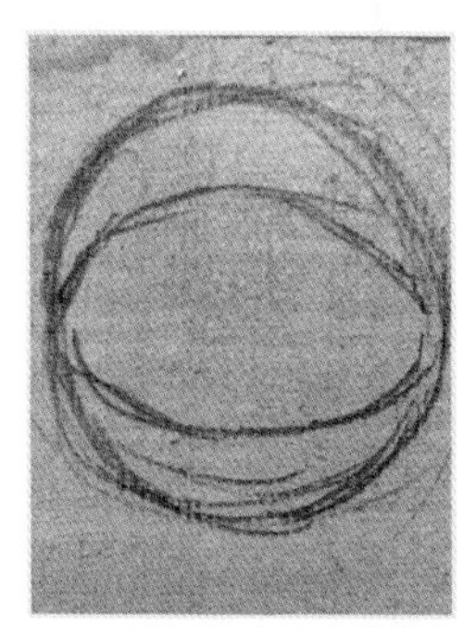

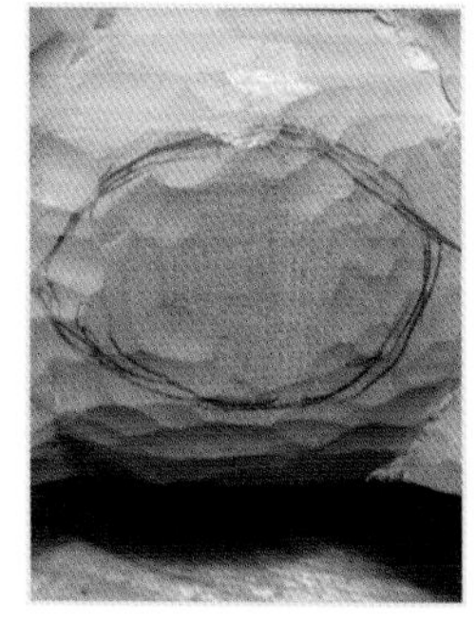

1 Draw the outline of the eyeball as if the eye was shut, then carve the bulge that it forms.

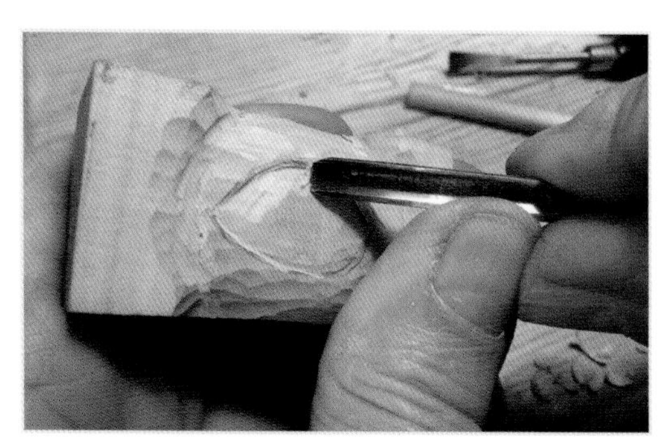

2 When you are happy with the form of the eyeball, draw in the eye outline. Bear in mind that the visible part of the eye is simply part of the sphere of the eyeball, so the curvature from left to right must be the same as that from top to bottom. Imagine cutting the shape of an eye out of the surface of an orange, then removing the peel. The flesh underneath represents the eyeball. A carved eye should look similar.

TIP: **A useful tip is to carve the eyes as if they were shut, before adding detail to show an open eye. All too often, carvers only see the open part of the eye, not the actual shape of the eyeball. Consequently, the eyes they carve inevitably turn out almond-shaped and bulging.**

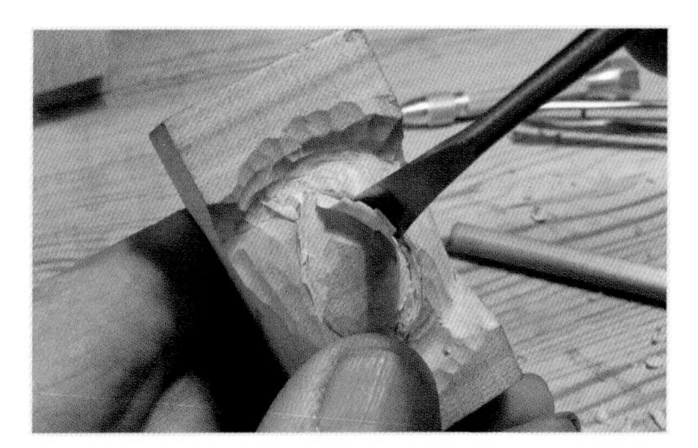

3 Cut the open part of the eye back into the mound. You can use whichever tool is most suitable to ensure that you finish with a smooth, clean, open part of the eye. Repeat the process for the second eye. It is essential that the eyes on both sides of the head match. Take your time doing this and check the position frequently.

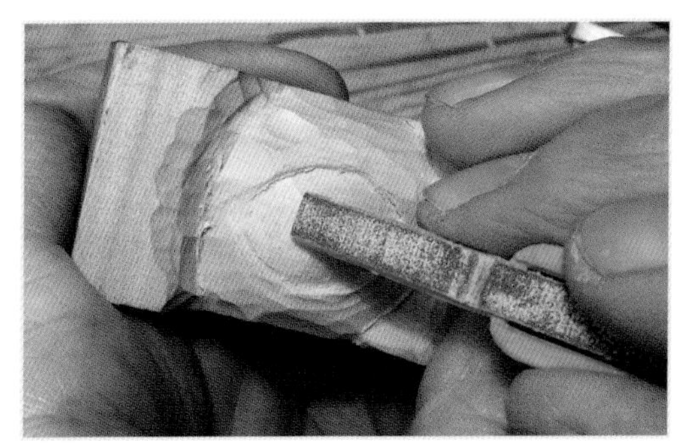

4 Once the eyes are carved you can either leave them as they are or paint them. Which method you choose depends on whether you want the eyes to look like the rest of the carving or more realistic. If you are going to paint them, make sure that the surface is absolutely smooth beforehand or it will never look right.

Painting carved eyes

This is actually very easy and often produces some amazingly realistic results.

5 Once the eye is sanded smooth, add a coat of sealer. I use an acrylic universal sealer, but you could also use a matt varnish or even PVA glue if you prefer.

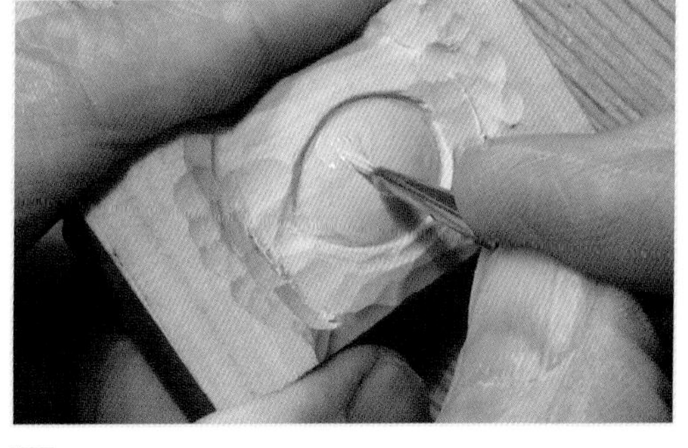

6 Next, give the whole eyeball a base coat. I tend to use yellow for this, but you might like to experiment. There are several types of paint you could use, although the easiest and most effective are water-based acrylics.

7 When the base coat is dry, start to add your chosen colours. Dilute the colours well and only add a little at a time.

8 Add as many coats of paint as you wish, gradually building up the colour. Remember that eyes are not a solid colour – they have all sorts of flecks in them.

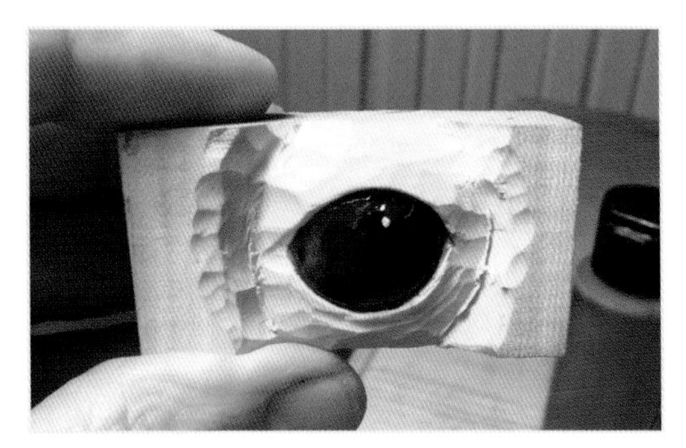

9 When you are happy with the general effect, start adding the gloss, letting a drop of clear nail varnish fall onto the surface of the eye gives a very satisfactory result. Avoid brushing it or you may lose the shiny surface. Add to this a small highlight with a speck of white paint if you wish. There are other ways of achieving the same result, but whichever method you choose, practice makes perfect.

TIP: **If you make the whole eye the same depth of colour, it will appear as if it is staring. When looking at a real eye, you will notice that there tends to be a shadow underneath the top eyelid, so try to shade the colour progressively darker as you go upwards.**

WARNING: **To minimize any damage to your carving, I recommend fitting the eyes as soon as possible, so that any finish can include the immediate surrounding area. You will need to leave any final polishing until all the carving is completed to avoid damage to the eyes. Ensure that you need to take great care fitting the eyes as you are unlikely to get a second chance.**

Making and inlaying eyes

A good inlaid eye can give an animal life and expression and really turn a netsuke into something special. There are many ways to do this. The method you choose will depend upon the available materials, as well as the size and the type of eye that is required. In order to demonstrate the procedure clearly, I have used practice pieces as they are larger than normal.

One colour

For very small carvings you might like to inlay a simple eye made from buffalo or ram's horn.

1 Carefully mark the location of each eye with a pencil.

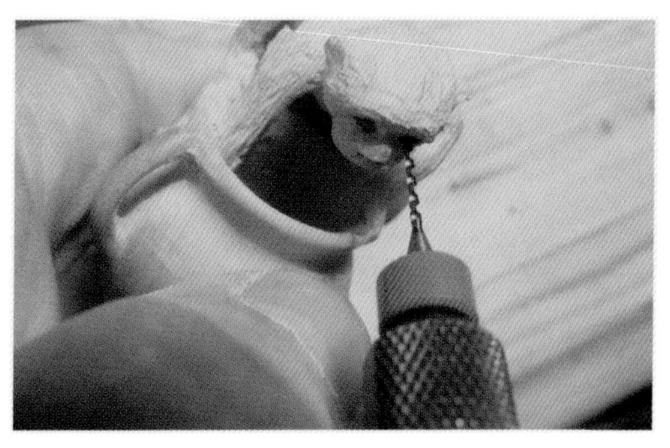

2 Drill two holes for the eyes in the carving and one in a spare piece of the same wood for the fitting. Drill a fine pilot hole first, then widen it. Avoid doing the preliminary fitting on the carving itself, as you could easily damage the socket.

3 Cut a small dowel from the horn and scrape or cut it down to the size of the fitting hole.

4 Once you have a good fit, fix the horn into the socket using a high-strength adhesive.

5 Repeat this process on the other eye, trimming off any surplus and sanding it down before polishing. When trimming down, cut small wedges until the surplus drops off. Do not try to break it off as horn has a grain and you could therefore lose part of the eye.

Two different colours

With larger eyes the process becomes more complicated, especially as there are several different methods you could use. To create the desired effect, you will also need to carefully source suitable materials. Amber or its substitutes, for example, can be used effectively for reptiles' and amphibians' eyes.

1 First, make a simple dowel and add a small dimple in the centre of the back. Paint this black to represent the pupil.

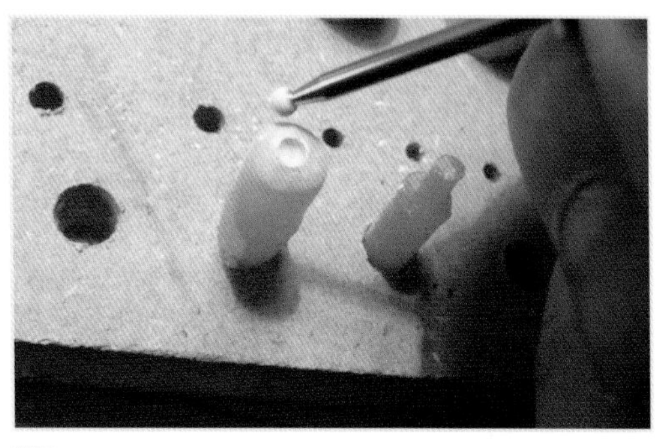

2 You can achieve a similar effect by drilling through the centre and inserting a different colour pupil. This works better when the eye material is not absolutely transparent, as it makes the pupil appear clearer.

3 If you wish to give the eye a slit-shaped pupil as opposed to a circular one, you will need to cut a right-angled V across the top of the dowel.

4 After cutting a piece of buffalo horn with a right-angled edge, fix this into the groove using high-strength adhesive. When this is secure it can be trimmed off and polished.

5 The shape of the slit pupil can be varied according to how you shape the eye. Here, the pupil is on the outside of the eye, whereas it was on the inside of the eye in the previous method.

Scales

If you are going to include fish, reptiles or amphibians in your collection of netsuke, you will need to learn how to carve various scales. Too often carvers assume that one type of scale fits any animal, yet the scales on each are markedly different. Ensuring your carving looks realistic requires thorough research, focusing particularly on the texture that is applicable. That said, we have to be realistic. Netsuke are very small, making it especially difficult to carve accurate scales on them. We therefore have to settle for producing an impression of scales.

Carving fish scales

In general, when carving scales on a fish you will probably end up creating a series of semicircular cuts in a diamond pattern, with each successive row overlapping the one following as you progress towards the tail.

1 First of all, carefully mark out all the scales you intend to carve. Do not attempt to carve them freehand, as you will almost certainly end up with a mess.

2 Next, use a small gouge or V tool to cut the scales. The best results are achieved by cutting the lines with the V tool resting on its side – that way you create a stepped effect, minimizing the amount of shaping you have to do. Make sure you have the stepping going down towards the tail. I have made this mistake before and ended up having to re-carve the whole piece.

3 Tidy up the outlines with a smaller V tool, then clean out the spaces between the scales with a skew chisel, a scalpel or something similar. Sand the piece down with fine abrasive paper, to leave an acceptable scale pattern. This will take a bit of practice to perfect.

Finished fish

Carving snake scales

Snake scales are much smaller than fish scales and do not overlap each other. When you reduce the snake to the size of a netsuke, its scales are minute and are therefore very difficult to produce. You can only make a representation and it would be a mistake to try to make it look like anything else.

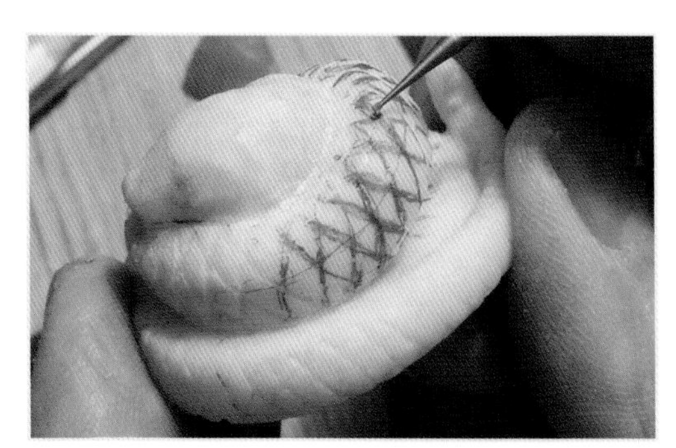

1 Cut a simple diagonal pattern as small as is practical and leave the viewer to interpret it. Draw the pattern on first to make sure that the lines are equally spaced and regular.

2 Cut the lines on the topside of the snake. However, remember that the underside is very different from the top. The pattern is in the form of parallel bands running from side to side.

Finished snake

TIP: How you make the patterns will vary according to the material you are using. With wood the best results will be achieved with cutting tools - either V tools or small veiners. If you are using horn, tagua or ivory, you may find a rotary burr much easier and effective. It is really a matter of trial and error.

Feathers

Any feathers you carve on a netsuke are bound to be very small; therefore, it is a good idea to practise on a larger version before carving such small details on miniature pieces. The example shown here is two or three times the size of the feathers needed for the turtle dove (see page 75). To get maximum value from practice pieces, you need to use the same timber as you are using for the netsuke, in this case pear wood. Look carefully at the shape and size of the feathers on a bird's wing. You do not need to copy them exactly, but try to get the general shape and relative size as accurate as you can.

1 First, cut a piece of waste wood and round it, so that it is similar to the bird shape you will be using. Mark out the main feather areas, focusing only on the primaries (big flight feathers), the secondaries (the smaller ones immediately above the primaries) and the coverts (the softer, smaller feathers that are closer to the ones on the rest of the body).

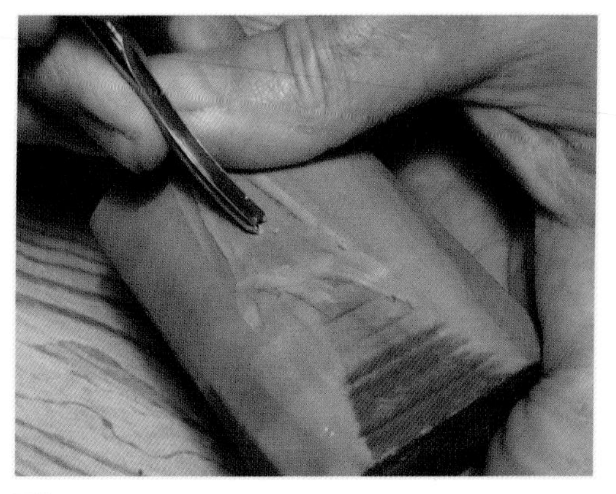

2 Profile these areas with a gouge or rotary burr, to ensure that you end up with a flat area for the primaries and two soft bumps for the other feathers.

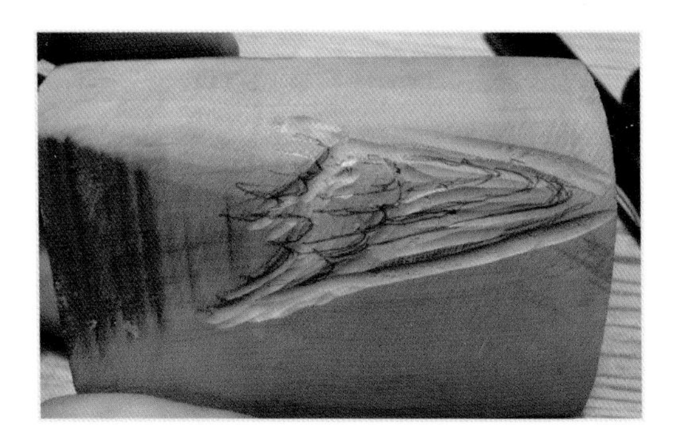

3 Once you are happy with the shape, draw on the feathers that you are going to carve. You may need several tries at this before you achieve the desired result, but it is important that you draw the feathers correctly before you start to carve. Never try carving them freehand, as they inevitably end up going all over the place.

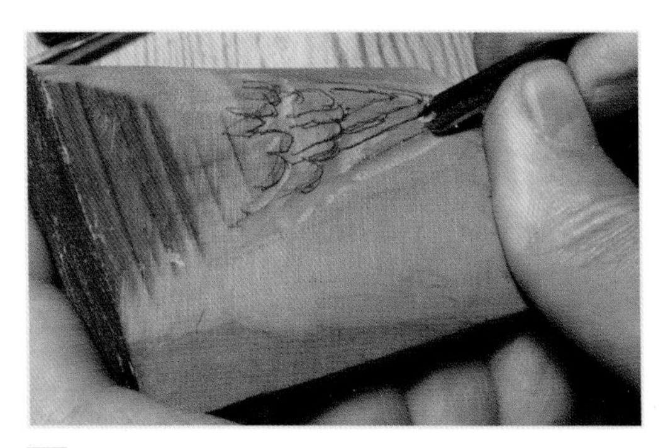

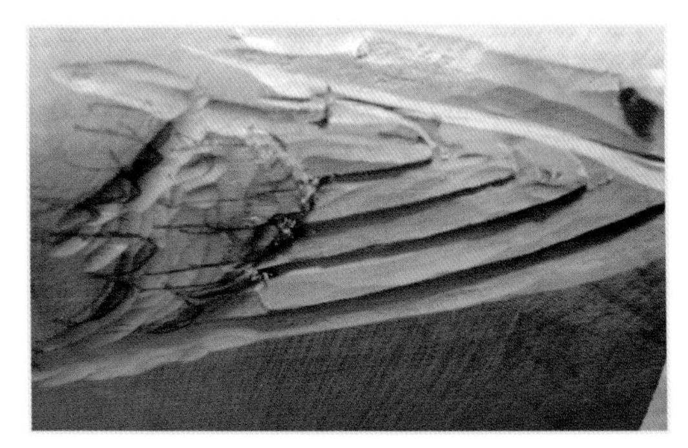

4 Using a V tool bigger than the flat area of the feathers – so no unwanted grooves appear on the surface – cut along the line of each primary feather, keeping one side of the V tool flat on the surface. It is important to remember throughout the process that as you work upwards towards the centre of the back, each successive feather rests on the one below it – rather like tiles on a roof. I have seen many netsuke birds with their feathers carved back to front.

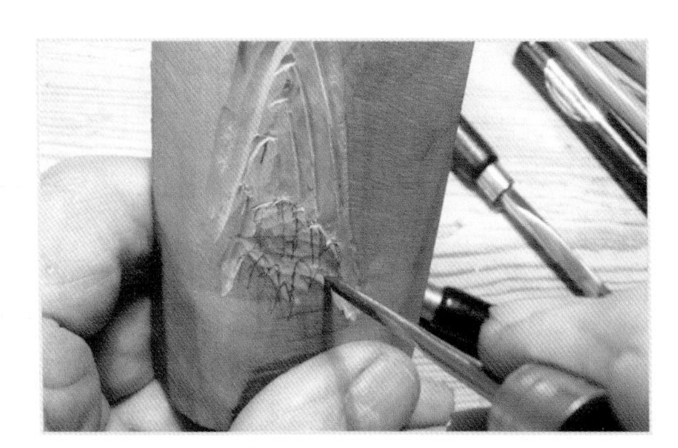

5 To carve the secondaries, go round the edge of each feather with a small gouge to achieve a clean curve. Clean out the areas between these and the primaries with the tip of a knife or scalpel. Again, the feathers overlap in the same way.

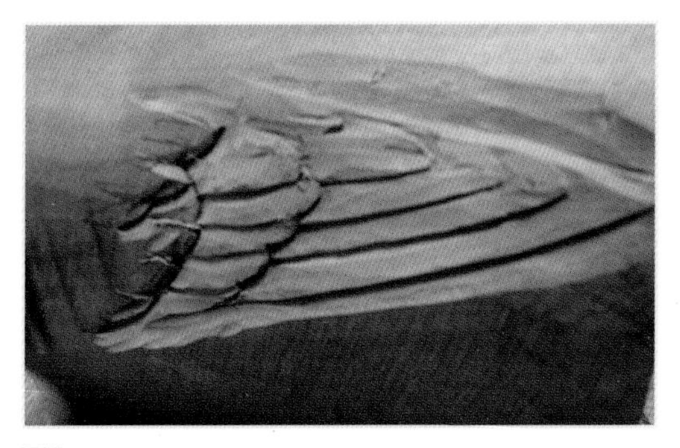

6 Repeat the process with the coverts until all the feathers are completed. How far you continue towards the head of the bird is up to you, but be careful not to overdo it. Now, give the whole piece a good clean and sand off any rough edges, making sure that the surface of the primaries is nice and flat.

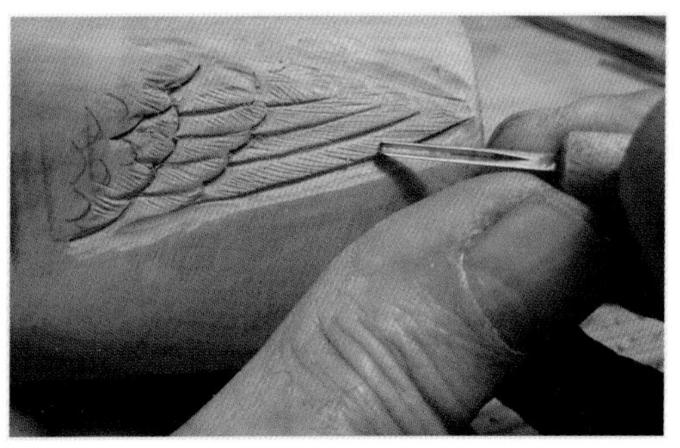

7 Add some texture to the feathers with a small V tool. I have added some very fine lines to show the structure of the feathers; these must be very fine. If you have a fine-point pyrograph tool, you can turn the heat right down to achieve the same effect or even finer lines. If you have any doubts about adding these lines, leave them out.

TIP: **If you are still not confident that you could repeat the process at 1/3 of the size, practise with another larger piece before tackling the netsuke. Never experiment directly on your carving, it is a certain recipe for disaster – always use your maquette or a practice piece.**

Finished turtle dove

Fur and hair

Adding fur or hair texture to something as small as a netsuke is relatively difficult. We certainly cannot make it look realistic, as hair is very fine in real life, let alone on a carving a fraction of the size. The best we can hope to produce is a realistic impression of hair.

1 Before you start, remove all pencil or ink marks left on the wood. You will not be able to alter the surface once you have completed the carving without spoiling the effect. It is also important to ensure that you know exactly what effect you intend to create and in which direction the fur runs for accurate representation.

2 For the process itself you will need some very fine tools; a 1/16 veiner and a 1/16 V tool are ideal. Make sure your tools are sharp and that they produce clean, crisp cuts. There is little hope of cleaning up any rough areas. A fine veiner tends to give a softer effect than a V tool, although this will create a finer effect. If you find it difficult to see where you have worked, you might also find it helpful to use a magnifier.

3 The basis of hair or fur carving is a long shallow 'S' in the direction you require, either up or down. This will avoid the straw effect that occurs when you carve straight lines. Remove only a very small amount of wood with each cut.

4 The most important thing to do is to keep practising until you can complete the whole process confidently. The faster you cut the better, as you will achieve a much more natural, lifelike effect. If you cannot achieve the right effect on your practice block, try again until you do, as it will be far more difficult on the carving itself.

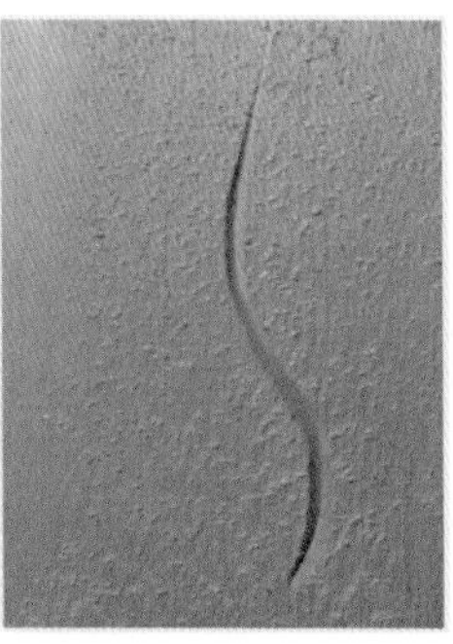

Single hair

Cluster of hairs

Finished rabbit

Ukibori

This technique is used to create raised bumps on carvings. These small bumps can be used in a wide variety of ways: raised veins on hands, warts on frogs and toads, the bumpy surface of snails, seams on clothing and even raised lettering. Achieving these results is actually very simple, when you know what you are doing. I have used boxwood for this illustration, as this is what I have carved with more than anything else; however, the process can be applied to almost any timber.

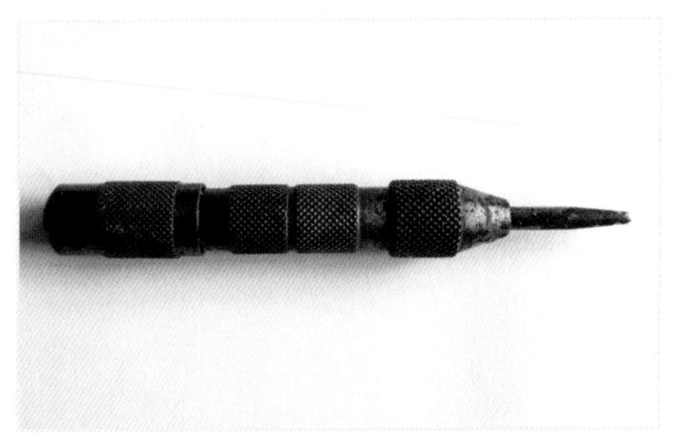

1 To start, you will need a small round-ended punch. Ensure that the end is absolutely smooth when polished, to prevent the fibres of the wood from being damaged.

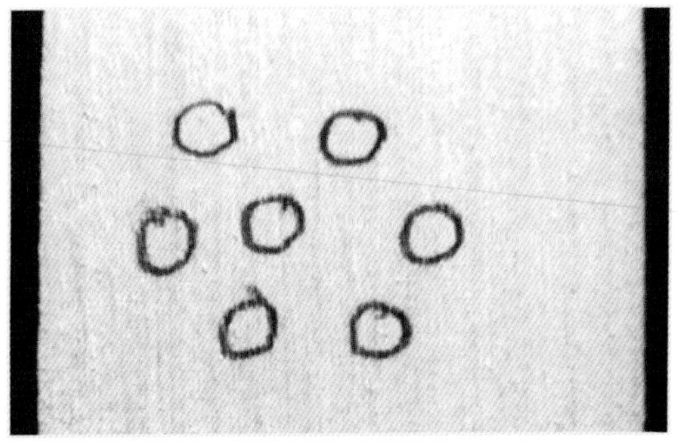

2 Decide where the bumps are going to be, then draw small rings to define where you are going to punch. Do not use a felt-tip pen as it may stain the wood.

3 Punch a dent in the surface using a small mallet or hammer, taking care not to break any of the surface fibres. I use an automatic centre punch that is spring loaded. This tool is easier to control, particularly if you are looking for dents of varying sizes. Sand or cut off the surface to the depth of the dents, to ensure that the whole surface is smooth.

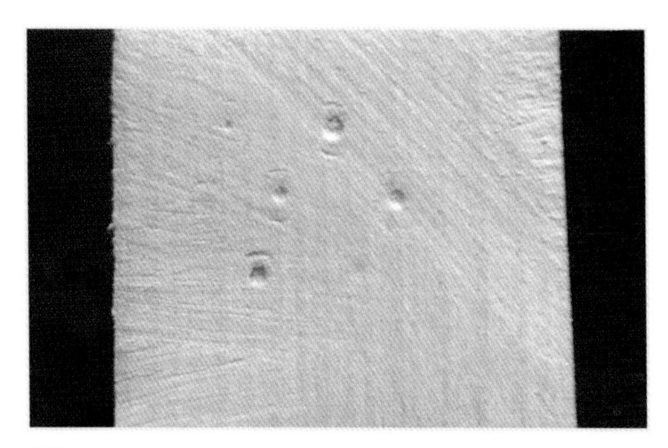

4 I have left the sanding a little short of the bottom of the dents to show where they are. On your carving, make sure that you go far enough for the dents to disappear. Wet the surface, so that all the dents swell to leave the surface covered in bumps. You will notice that some of the bumps have little hollows in the top. These are dents that were not quite sanded down.

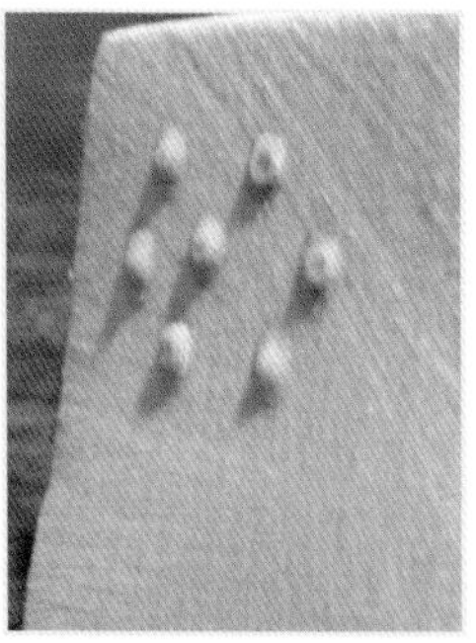

5 Any irregularities created during the punching will be repeated after the wetting; therefore, it is important to take the time to practise this technique before you start hammering your carving. Different woods respond in different ways, so practise on the same wood as your carving.

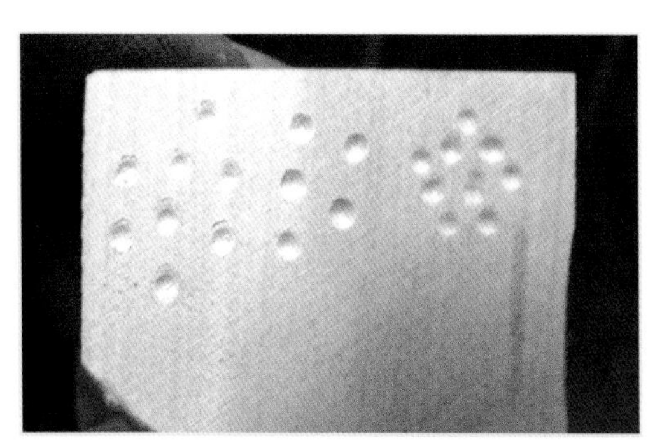

6 If you are looking to create bumps of different sizes on the same carving, the process is a little more complicated. Punch the largest bumps first and partly sand. Then, start on the second set, the bottom of which should be at the same level as the bottom of the first set. Part sand and punch again, once more to the same level as the other two sets. When you sand off the wood around the dents, you should reach the bottom of all the different-sized dents, leaving the surface smooth.

7 When you wet the surface, you should have three different-sized bumps. You can, of course, apply this process as many times as you wish. However, you will need to use a selection of various-sized punches to achieve a wider range of sizes.

Different shapes

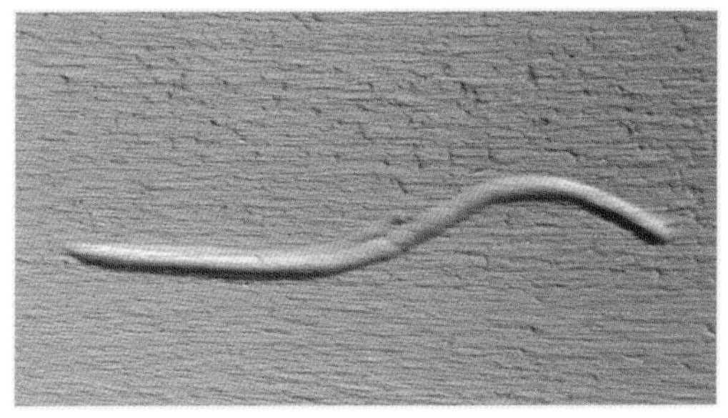

1 To use this technique to create either seams or bumps of different shapes, slide or push the end of the punch along the surface of the wood. This will make dents of the shape you require.

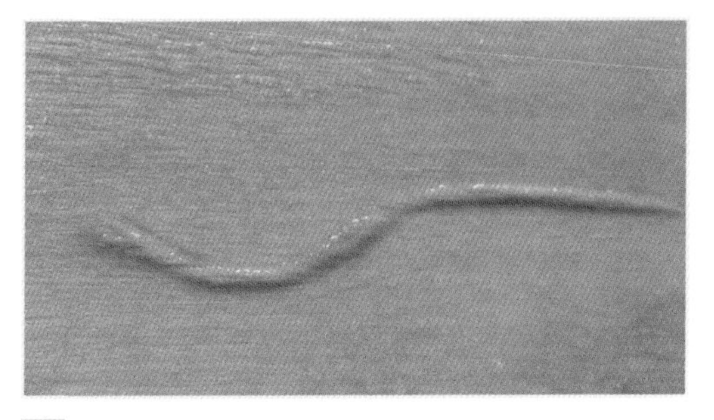

2 Make sure that any sanding you do to the surface is done with a fine abrasive before wetting, as you cannot do anything more to this surface afterwards. These imperfections will therefore remain in the final result.

The photos below show this technique applied to a larger carving in lime of a dancer in a leotard.

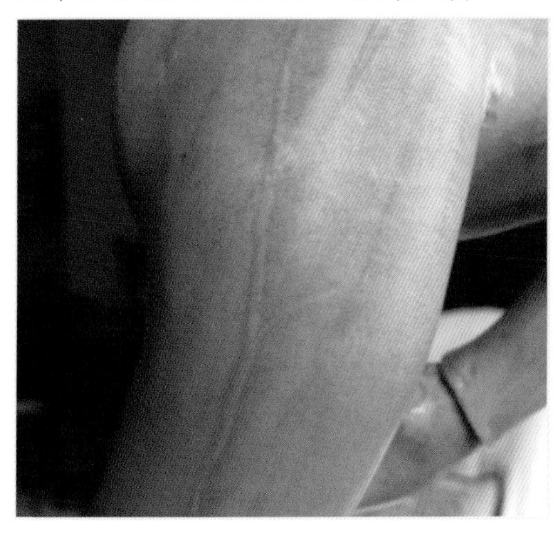

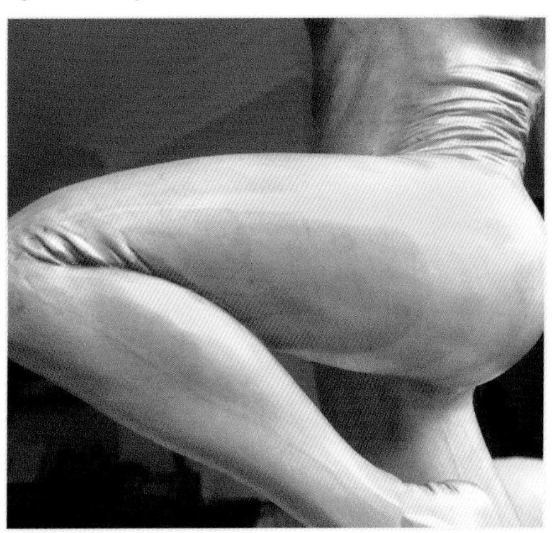

TIP: Even after you have practised the process, you may well find that you do not get it right first time. Do not worry; you can repeat the process even over a small part of the original area. There are limits, of course, as you may eventually run out of wood.

Adding colour

There are dozens of different ways to add colour to your carvings. I will try to cover as many as I can in this section, concentrating on those I have used myself. These will be broken down into ones you can purchase in your local shop and those you can make yourself, find or modify.

Wood stain

The method most carvers first consider is a proprietary wood stain of some sort. These work well, but they are difficult to control as the colour often runs. It will also appear darker on end grain than it will on long grain. As all netsuke will be quite a complicated combination of both, you may well end up with a very patchy finish. Having said that, if you can control it, wood stain can be used to good effect, so do not dismiss it entirely.

Paints

For a very detailed colour finish involving many different colours, you are best using paints. Although there seems to be a strong aversion to the use of paint on carvings, many of the classical sculptures, both wood and marble, would have been coloured with bright paints.

With the development of modern pigments and solvents, there is now a wide choice of paints available. I prefer to use acrylic, water-based paints as they are easy to manage. By diluting them you can add a light wash to your work, which can be built up to achieve brighter colours.

Dyes

Water-based paints can be difficult to use when working with very hard woods or other materials, as the colour tends to sit on the surface. Another option is to use dyes. Take a good look at the choices available and try out several different ones.

A simple hot-water fabric dye is very effective on hardwoods. This will require courage as it involves plunging your carving into boiling water into which the powdered dye has already been added. Only leave your work submerged in the water for around 40 seconds, then take it out and immediately place it in cold water to cool down. Once cool, pat it dry then leave it to dry off naturally. Try experimenting with the same dye in the cold-water version.

If you want to leave any areas undyed, mask these off with a latex solution. Once the carving has dried, any masking can be peeled off to reveal areas of natural wood colour. You can create stunning netsuke using this technique, particularly with animals as you can dye the main body of the animal, while leaving its face, hands and feet as natural wood.

There are also many natural dyes that work well on most materials, including ivory, horn and bone. Tea and coffee have been extensively applied to produce subtle effects. Beetroot, walnut juice and onion can also add beautiful colours to your work.

Chemicals

There are several chemical treatments that will change the colour of your carving, some easier to use than others. Boxwood, in particular, can be taken from its natural colour through the various shades of brown to black by fuming it with concentrated nitric acid. Although only use this method with a proper fume cupboard!

Potassium permanganate produces a very rich brown colour as it dries. When this is first applied, it is a bright reddish purple colour. I suggest practising on a spare piece of wood beforehand, so that the initial colour is not so shocking.

An easier and probably more suitable method of darkening wooden carvings is to use vinegar. Drop a small amount of fine wire wool into a jar of vinegar and leave it to soak for about a week. After this time the wire wool will have virtually disappeared, leaving a rather dirty-looking solution. Apply this to your wood and it will turn grey – some woods greyer than others. This is because the solution reacts with the tannin in the wood. To make the colour darker, increase the tannin by applying an old wet tea bag. With repeated applications you can attain almost jet-black wood.

An advantage of this method is that you can paint the solution on and maintain a straight line or edge without the need to mask off any areas. If you do not like the smell, use cola instead of vinegar. It takes slightly longer, but works just as well.

All of the above assumes that the carver wishes to colour or darken the carving. However, in some cases, you may want to lighten the netsuke, either completely or isolated parts of it.

Bleach

There are several products that can bleach or lighten wood. In my opinion, nothing beats the two-part wood bleach, available from specialist suppliers (see page 158 for details).

The A solution is applied to the wood and left for around ten minutes. After this, the B solution is added and left for up to two hours, depending on how light you want the final result to be. The carving is then washed thoroughly in clean water and left to dry. All these instructions are written on the product. They may vary depending on the manufacturer, so read them carefully.

When a carving has been bleached you may not want to add a finish, as this could darken the colour. The only treatment I have found that keeps it close to white is a light spray with a clear acrylic aerosol lacquer. This is easily purchased from a car-accessory or arts and craft shop. If you only put a thin coat on each time, there should be no problems with the grain lifting.

Wire wool used to darken wood

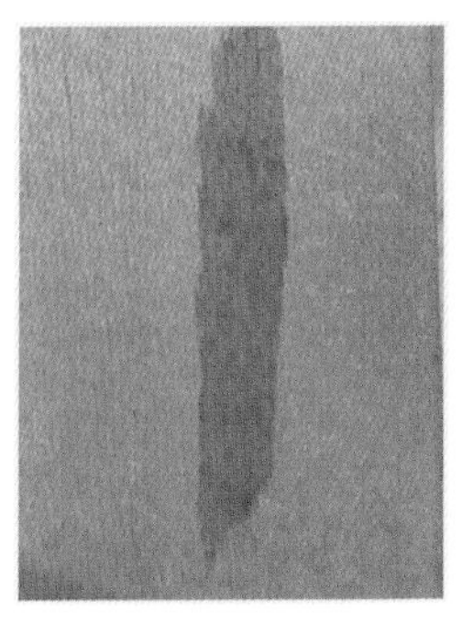

Vinegar solution added

Increasing the depth of colour

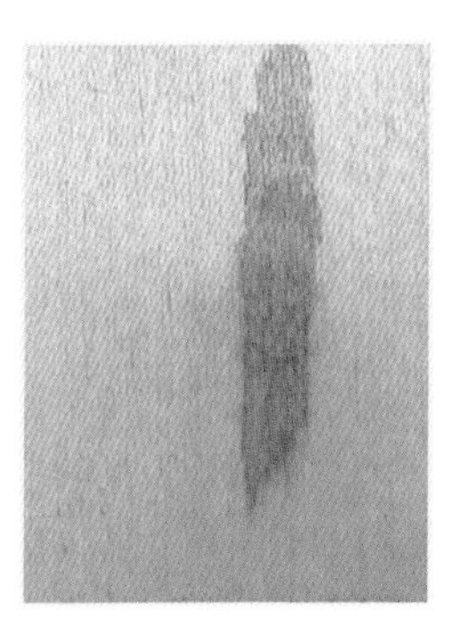

The resulting darkened wood

Himotoshi

The *himotoshi* is simply two holes joined by a tunnel. The cord from the *sagemono* goes in one side and out the other. One of these holes is generally, although not always, larger than the other so that it can contain the knot in the cord. It is important to place the *himotoshi* in such a position that, when held in place on the top of the *obi* by the cord, the netsuke sits in the correct position. The space between the two holes makes a convenient spot to place your signature or initials.

The *netsuke-shi* use the *himotoshi* as an extra chance to demonstrate their expertise. There are several different ways to enhance a *himotoshi*. The easiest method is to line the holes with some kind of simple inlay. When carving the toad (on page 100) I decided to use ram's horn. This process is detailed below. However, it is not essential to include a *himotoshi*, as long as there is some provision for the cord to enter and leave the netsuke; many netsuke do not have one at all.

1 Any sort of inlay material will become very fragile when cut to size, therefore, drill the holes while the material is still in a reasonably sized lump.

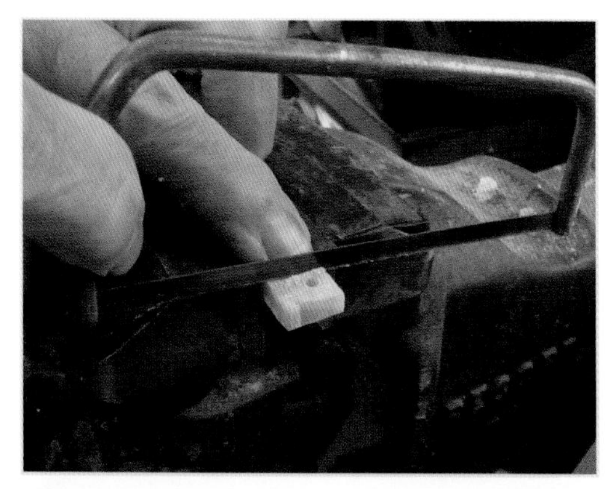

2 Cut the piece with the hole in it roughly into shape using a mini hacksaw. Leave plenty of material around the hole to avoid breakage.

TIP: When fitting the inserts, there is always the chance that they may jam in the holes, and in trying to remove them you could damage the carving. One tip is to drill a duplicate pair of holes in a piece of spare timber of the same type as the carving.

3 Drill the holes in your carving to the size you want your inlay to be. Join these up using a rotary burr. Alternatively, use a small veiner, leaving a shelf about 1/16in (2mm) down from the surface for the inlay to rest on.

4 Mount the piece of horn onto a small mandrel fitted into a rotary power carver, then turn it to shape by running it against some coarse cloth-backed abrasive.

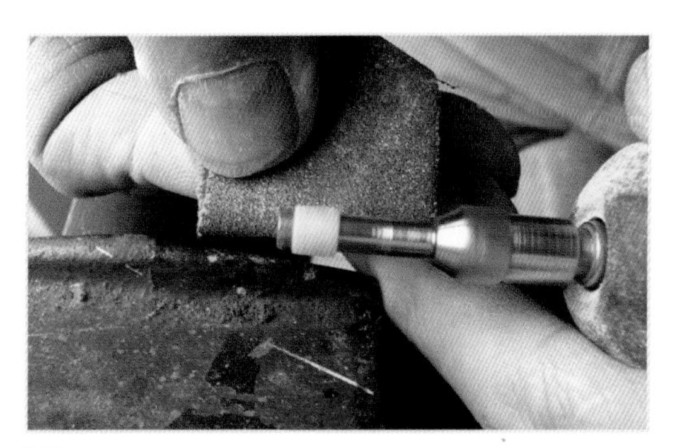

5 When the block of horn is cylindrical in shape, start to fit it to the holes. Repeat the turning process with finer abrasives or shape the horn by hand until the inserts in the spare wood are a snug fit.

6 Next, glue them into the holes you have cut in your carving using high-strength adhesive. Rub the inserts down until they are flush, then polish them. This will give you very neat *himotoshi* that are slightly different. You can use a wide range of materials in just the same way.

TIP: Another option is to make the whole *himotoshi* out of a different material from the rest of the carving. The ivory carving of the apple starting on page 118 uses a single horn inlay for both of the holes. The same basic making and fitting process applies as for those described above.

PROJECTS

DORMOUSE

A ball or sphere is the simplest shape within which to carve a netsuke, so lets start with a subject that is most easily suited to this shape: a curled-up dormouse. This is a fairly common subject with many pictures available for reference.

DORMOUSE

Toolbox

You will need the following:

Full-sized gouges:

1/4in (6mm) number 3
1/4in (6mm) number 9

Palm tools or block cutters:

1/8in (3mm) number 3
1/16in (1.5mm) number 39 V tool
3/16in (4.5mm) number 9
1/8in (3mm) number 3
1/16in (1.5mm) veiner

Additional:

Plasticine
Small knife and/or scalpel
Abrasive, probably no coarser than 120 grit

If using power tools when roughing out:

Sintered carbide cutter for the heaviest work
Cylindrical or conical burr for the finer work

NB: I would still recommend that the fine details are carved using hand tools.

Materials

Almost any timber that will take fine detail would be suitable for this project; yet many of these woods are very hard in texture and can therefore be difficult to work with.

I have chosen lime, as the detailed work is not too fine and the wood is comparatively easy to work. Lime can also provide quite an attractive grain pattern. However, feel free to use another timber if you prefer.

You will need a piece about 1 3/4in (44.5mm) square and 3in or 4in (76mm or 100mm) long. The increased length gives you something to hold onto while you are carving. It is difficult to carve something this small when you are having to hold it in your fingertips.

Creating the maquette

The pictures below show the maquette from all sides, so you can make up patterns from any angle.

As this project is based around a ball shape, the obvious starting point is to make up a ball of plasticine of a suitable size. Do not worry about making it the size of your finished dormouse, as you may not have decided at this stage exactly how large or small it is going to be. The picture below shows two alternative sizes, for example. Identify where the various parts of the animal should go using your reference pictures as a guide. Then start to model these features in the plasticine or modelling clay. You might like to carve it to get the feel of the shaping process.

TIP: **This stage of the project is really so that you can get the feel of the animal and its shape. Do not worry about the detail. You can always go back to the maquette later if you are unsure about anything. It should be a working model, which develops alongside your carving.**

Producing the basic shape

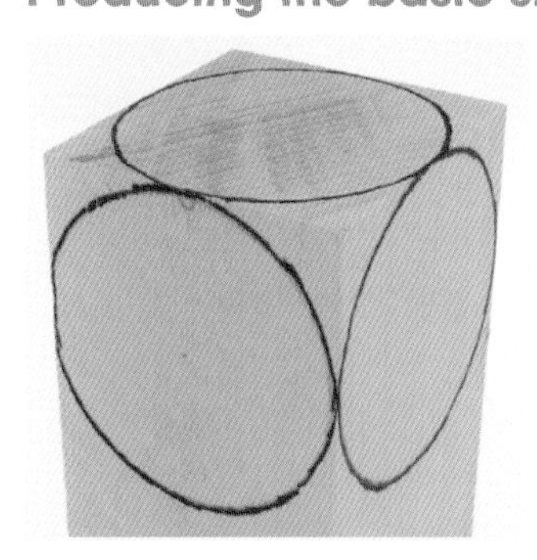

1 Once the maquette is completed and you are happy with the shape, you can start moulding the ball. Mark this on the end of your piece of wood.

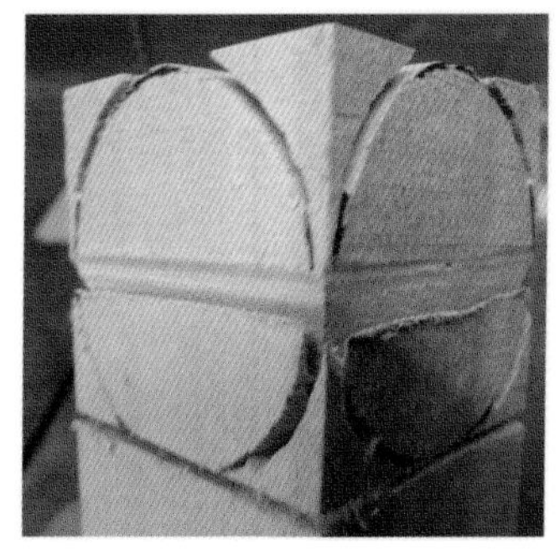

2 It is easier to cut these out using a bandsaw or coping saw, but it is also possible to do so using hand tools.

3 This process will give you a circle with corners.

4 Start to cut off the corners in order to produce the ball shape. A number 3 gouge is a useful tool for this, as it can cover the basic rounding of the top, as well as the undercutting for the bottom.

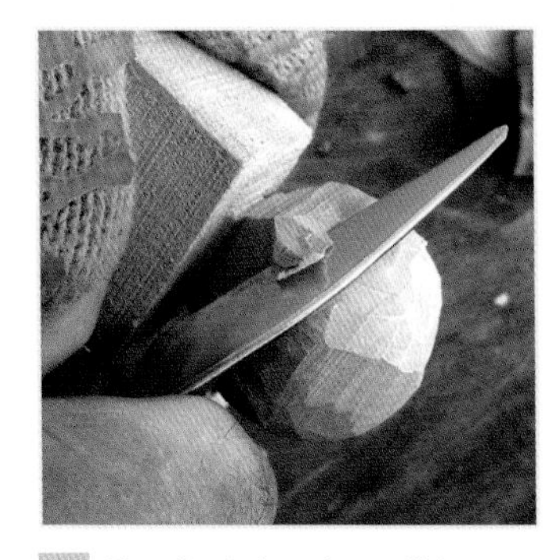

5 The final shaping will be easiest with a knife, but do not forget your safety glove!

6 Using full-sized gouges, make a ball shape by hand while holding the block in a vice. The shape does not need to be entirely accurate, just roughly spherical. If you have a lathe you could, of course, turn a small ball on the end of your block to reduce the carving time.

Setting out the figure

7 Draw a centre line from the base of one side, up and over the top and down to the base of the other side. This represents the line of symmetry of the animal that runs along the spine, between the ears and eyes, down the nose and down the centre of the front of the body. This is the datum line from which we measure and check all the detail and the symmetry.

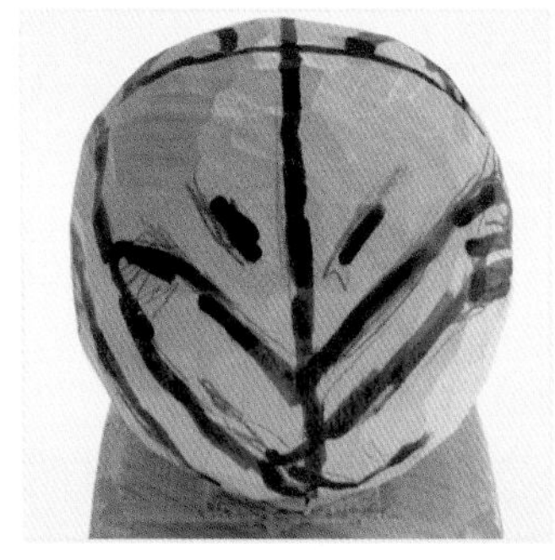

8 Using this line as a guide, mark out the relevant parts – ears, arms, legs and so on. Ensure that you locate the top of the head at the end of the stick – that is with the grain running vertically through the figure. Do not worry about the actual detail at this point, just the location. The aim is to apportion the wood that you will need for each part.

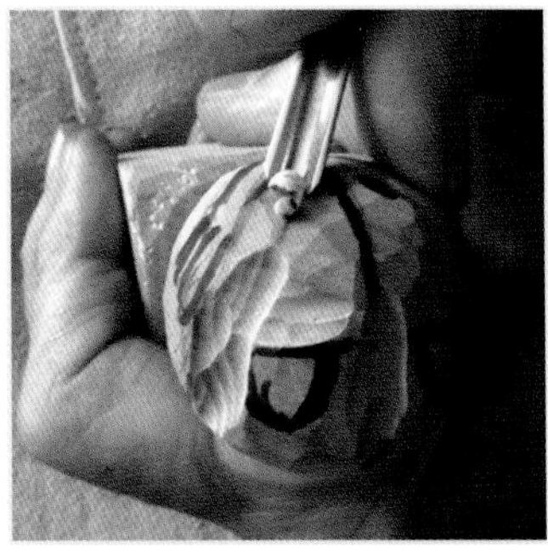

9 Starting with the top of the head, remove any obvious surplus wood, making sure that you leave enough wood for the ears. A $^{3}/_{16}$in (4.5mm) number 9 blockcutter is the most suitable tool with which to do this, as it removes the waste without damaging either side. Any ripple effect that occurs can be removed later on.

Getting the limbs right

10 This is the basic form of the subject. The finer details can be added later. Check thoroughly for symmetry. Any important reference points should be marked at this stage, such as the pelvis, as shown, the shoulders and so on.

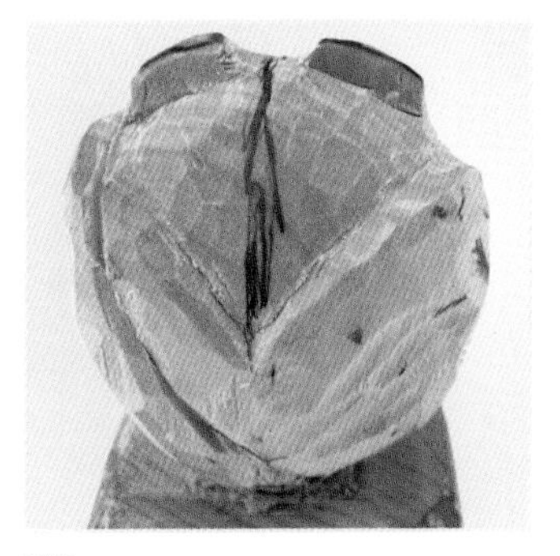

11 Next, draw in the arms and legs, ensuring that you carve them in the correct places. Simple centre lines can be used to indicate the right position.

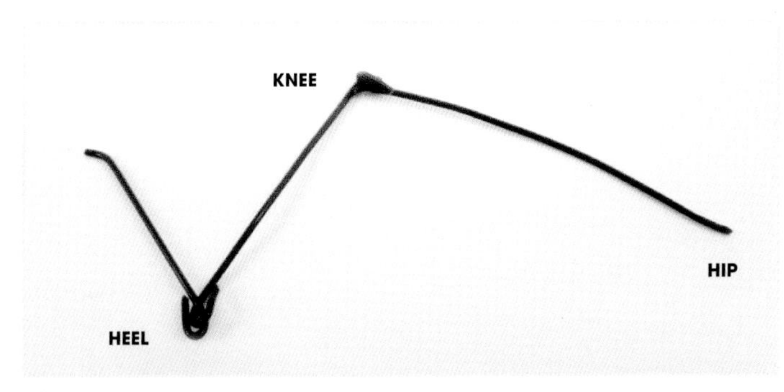

12 You might like to make up wire guides to help here. These are just pieces of thin wire of the correct length for an arm and others for a leg, joined together with loops at one end. These can be positioned and moved until you are satisfied.

TIP: Although the aim is to get all the proportions right, these are often difficult to determine with some animals. In addition, netsuke carving is more about capturing the essence of the subject rather than its anatomical accuracy. Therefore, it is more important to ensure that the limbs match on both sides, whatever their length.

13 Locate the hip end of your guide to a point on the pelvis and place the wire on the leg area – this is not critical as long as the point chosen matches on both sides. By adjusting the wire you should be able to determine the positions of the knee, heel and foot.

14 Once you are satisfied that the various limbs are where you want them, including the elbows and knees, you can start to refine some of the detail. The finer detail will be added later. However, the figure should be recognizable as a dormouse.

TIP: Remember that this is a soft, furry animal and this should be reflected in your work. It should have soft outlines all over with no sharp edges.

Smoothing off

Before you add any fine details, I suggest that you get the whole shape as smooth as possible. Smoothing off the wood means removing any imperfections that might change some area of the shape. At this stage, you are only really focusing on getting rid of any major defects. You can perfect the surface later on. Smoothing the wood at this stage also means that you know exactly how much wood you have for the final detailing.

15 There are many abrasive cloths and papers on the market. Start with a grade that is as fine as you think you need, then go through the grades, getting finer and finer, until you attain the required result. Alternatively, you can use a really sharp knife or gouge to gradually smooth the surface, finally scraping away any residual tool marks. By the time you have finished, there should be no sign of any scratches on your work, even if you intend to add texture to the piece later on.

Adding detail

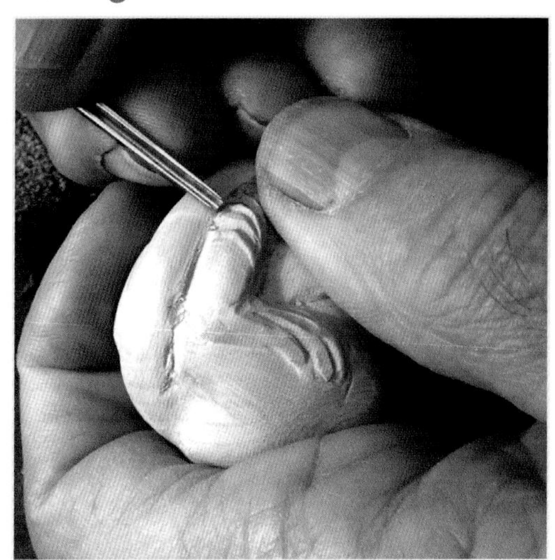

16 When you are happy with the first stage of the smoothing process, you can add the fine detail, starting with the fingers and toes. Rodents usually have four fingers and five toes. (There will always be someone who knows this and will point it out if you carve it wrong.) The carving is best done with a 1/16in (1.5mm) V tool. This is also a good time to remove the mouse from the supporting block. Be careful not to cut too high in case you lose the ball shape.

TIP: Draw the detail with a pencil and do not start to carve until you are happy with it. Once you start, stick to the lines you have drawn. Carving such detail freehand is very seldom successful.

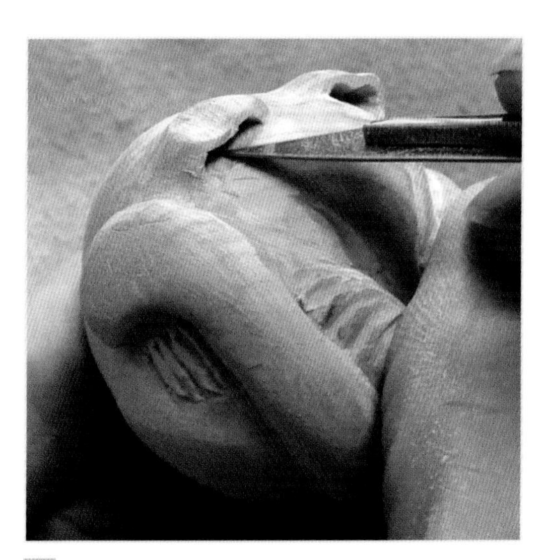

17 The ears need to be shaped on the outside before you attempt to hollow them out. When you are happy with the shape, carefully cut inside each one with a scalpel, making sure that you do not break away the fine edge you are cutting.

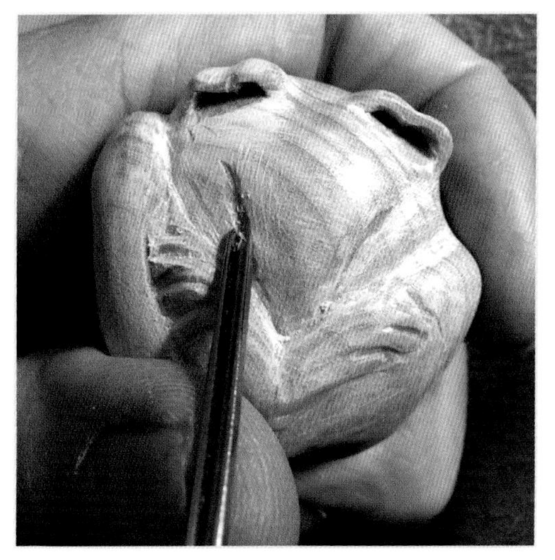

18 Do not attempt to carve complete eyes – the figure is far too small. The dormouse is asleep, so its eyes will be shut and can be represented by small, curved slits. Just make sure that you carve them in the right place – check and check again. You might prefer to make your initial cuts with the fine V tool, but you will find that a final deep cut with a knife or scalpel will improve the appearance.

19 Although this is a netsuke, and is therefore designed to be primarily a functional item, it still has to be displayed in the correct position. Therefore, carve the bottom until it is flat.

20 Sand the whole piece thoroughly before the last stage. Your basic carving is now almost finished. The shape is completed, but it is still not quite a netsuke yet.

TIP: At this stage, it is a good idea to check that all the surfaces are really clean and smooth, and that all detail cuts are crisps with no 'fuzzies'.

Adding the himotoshi

21 Using a drill of about 1/6in (4mm), drill two holes in the flat area about 1/2in (12mm) apart.

22 Carefully join these holes together using your curved 1/16in (1.5mm) veiner. If you are using power tools, a small ball-shaped burr is very useful for this job.

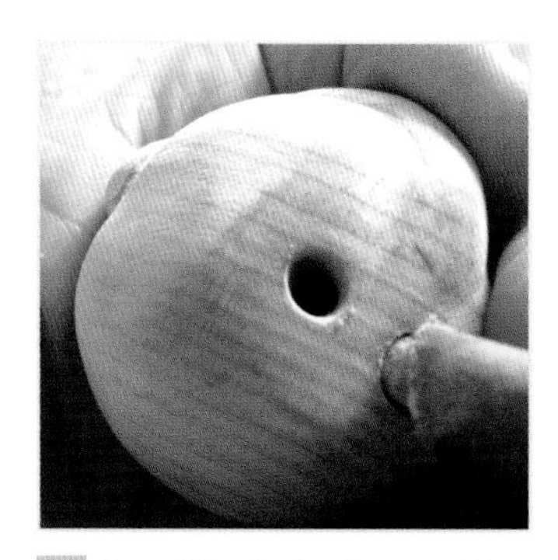

23 Sand the holes thoroughly, making sure that there are no rough edges. One hole should be a little larger than the other to accommodate the knot in the cord that is inserted.

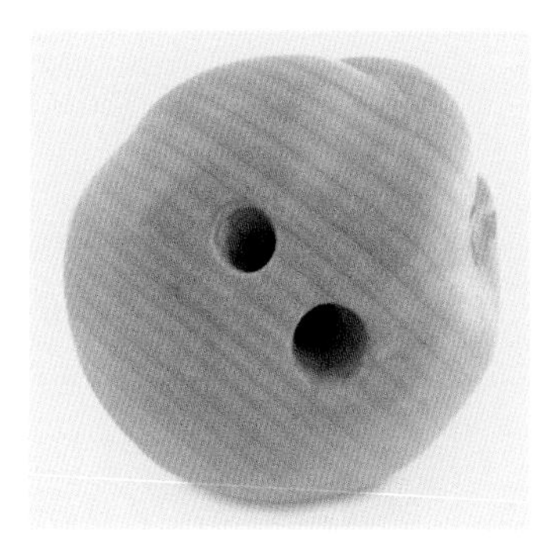

24 You have now finished the carving. I am not going to add fur texture to this piece, but should you wish to do so I suggest that you study the rabbit starting on page 78, as well as the section on carving fur on page 50. Lime is not ideal for this kind of detail on a carving of this size, but if you have used another type of wood with a very fine grain it may work.

Finishing

To truly appreciate the form and character of the carving, netsuke really need to be handled; therefore, I rarely use a wax finish as this can get dirty and sticky with handling. Instead I favour a finishing oil of some kind. There are many of these on the market, and every carver has a favourite. I generally use either Tung oil or Danish oil, but the choice is yours.

25 Apply several coats of oil and rub it in well, making sure that you do not leave any surplus on the surface. When this is dry, it can be easily wiped over with a damp cloth should the carving need to be cleaned.

TURTLE DOVE

This piece is based on one of the most common starting shapes for a netsuke, an ovoid. An obvious subject for this shape is a bird, in this case a sleeping turtle dove. There is plenty of reference material available to study and often real-life examples close to home.

TURTLE DOVE

Toolbox

You will need the following:

Full-sized gouges:

1/4in (6mm) number 3
1/4in (6mm) number 9

Palm tools or block cutters:

1/8in (3mm) number 3
1/16in (1.5mm) number 39 V tool
1/16in (1.5mm) veiner
1/4in (6mm) number 3
3/16in (4.5mm) number 2 skew chisel

Additional:

Plasticine
Small knife and/or scalpel
A magnifier
A suitable holding device

Materials

You will need a piece of timber around 4in (100mm) in length by about 1 3/4in (44.5mm) square. Traditionally, wooden netsuke are carved in fruitwoods or boxwood as these are ideal for holding fine detail. I have chosen to use steamed pear wood as it has a beautiful colour, shows fine detail and carves easily. You may, of course, have your own preference.

Creating the maquette

The pictures below show the maquette from all sides, so you can make up patterns from any angle.

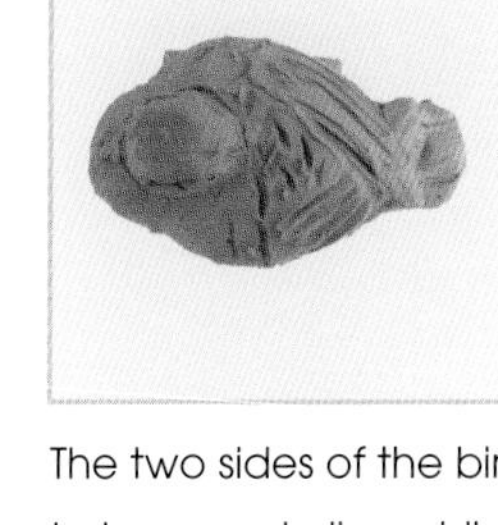

When making the maquette, look carefully at birds resting, either in real life or in photographs. Make a note of the elements that strike you. I have chosen to create a turtle dove, although my work is not an exact resemblance. The aim is to capture the essence of the bird and portray it in your own way, not to get too complicated or tied up with details.

The two sides of the bird are obviously going to be very similar, while the top can include any turn of the head you choose. Most importantly, ensure you look carefully at the balance of the piece. The bird should not be tipping forward or backwards, nor leaning left or right.

Producing the basic shape

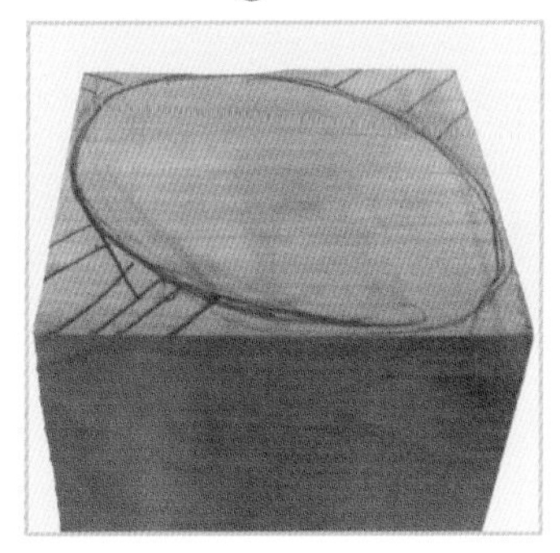

1 When you are happy with your maquette, mark the largest oval possible on the top of your block, then secure the block in a small vice. As this wood is pretty hard, you will find it difficult to work with if you are holding it in your hand.

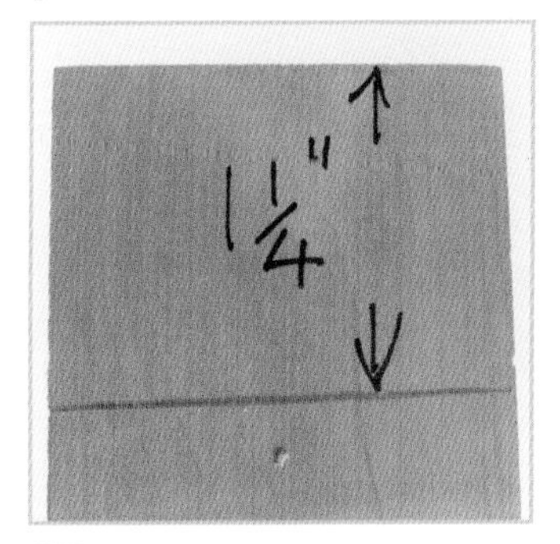

2 Measure down around 1¼in (32mm) and draw a line all round the block.

3 Cut this line about ¼in (6mm) deep with either a bandsaw or a hand saw to mark the bottom of your carving block.

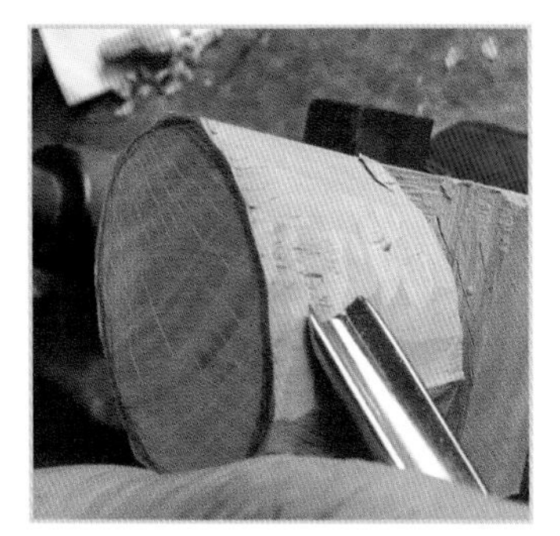

4 Using a number 3 gouge, cut down to the base around the oval you have marked out to create an oval cylinder shape. You may need to use a mallet for this.

5 Pear tends to have a rather wild grain, so be careful that the cut does not go out of control. If you have a problem, cut across the grain with your number 9 gouge.

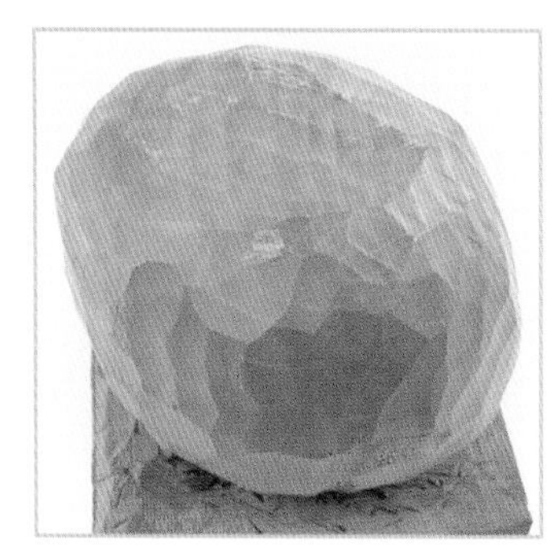

6 When you are satisfied with the shape, round it off at both the top and the bottom with your number 3 gouge. It is worth noting that this is the most wood you will be removing throughout the whole project.

Mark in the head

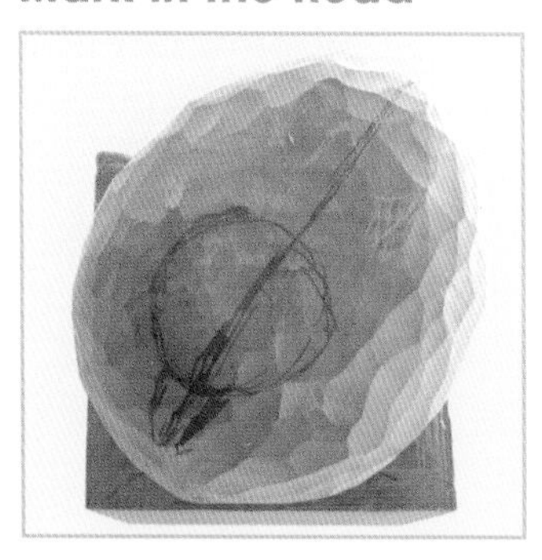

7 Draw the position of the head on the top of the block, so that you can see where you need to leave wood. If you wish to change the position of the head from that shown in your maquette, do so now. You will not be able to do it further along the line.

Roughing out the figure

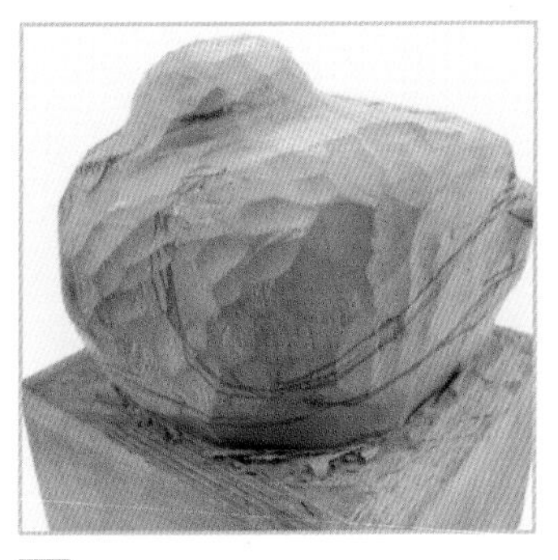

8 Reduce the level of the top of your oval, remembering to leave the head outline intact. Go down to around 1/4in (6mm), then round off the body again. The best tool for this is a 3/16in (5mm) number 9 blockcutter or a 1/4in (6mm) full-sized gouge – whichever tool you feel most comfortable with. From here on, it is usually easier to take the work out of the vice and to work with it in your hand.

9 Using the maquette as a guide, locate all the important parts of the bird's wings, chest, tail and so on. Then, draw these clearly on your block to provide the rough form of the bird.

10 Next, start to round off the head and the beak.

TIP: Although the aim is to get all the proportions right, these are often difficult to determine with some animals. In addition, netsuke carving is more about capturing the essence of the subject rather than its anatomical accuracy. Therefore, it is more important to ensure that the wings match on both sides, whatever their length.

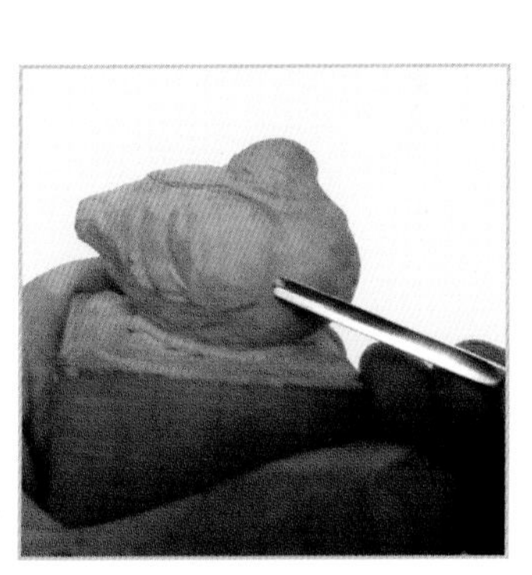

11 Draw on a more detailed outline, so that you can begin to shape your carving. Remember that birds are very soft, their feathers will give to any weight or pressure and their head sinks into the body feathers. So avoid hard edges or surfaces.

12 Use a gouge with a slight sweep to it, ideally a number 3, rather than a flat chisel to smooth the surfaces. At this stage, you are simply refining the overall shape of your bird without adding any real detail. Do not worry about the underside too much, as you can always take wood off here later on. It is better that your bird looks too fat rather than too thin.

Smoothing off

13 Now is a good time to sand the whole carving and to check the contours that you have carved by comparing them with pictures of birds. Bear in mind that rough or incorrectly formed areas will stand out much more on a carving as small as this. Therefore, spend as much time as possible getting this right before going through the grades of abrasive. If you do not intend to carve the feather detail, sand the piece to a finish, apart from the underside.

14 Remove the carving from its base using a bandsaw or a coping saw in order to finish the underside and to carve the feather detail. This will make the piece difficult to hold, but also more manoeuvrable for getting into all the little nooks and crannies.

Adding feather detail

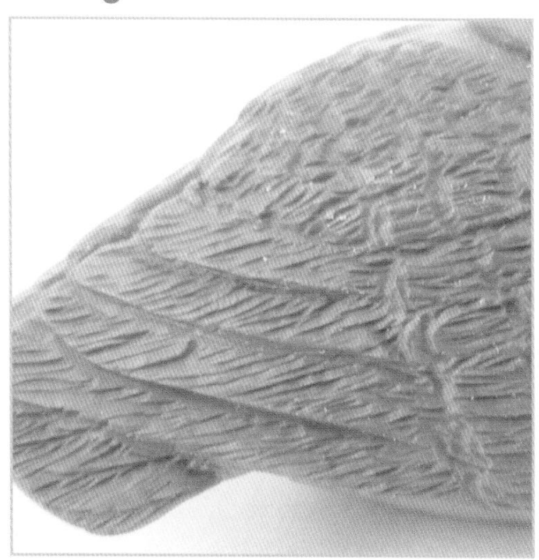

15 If you have never carved birds before, it is a good idea to practise carving feathers. When creating something this size, it is not important to get everything absolutely accurate. You need to know the various shapes of the feathers and how they overlap, but as long as you include the main types in the right places, the number of feathers is not really an issue.

NB: On something this small it is not possible to show the actual carving of the feathers in detail. To see the process in a larger form, refer to page 47.

16 When you are confident that you can carve the feathers on your dove, draw them in carefully with a fine pencil, before outlining them with your small V tool. Take your time doing this, as you will have limited opportunity to redo it.

Adding the himotoshi

17 Flatten the base of your dove, checking that it sits flat and does not lean to one side or the other. Refer to your research photographs to ensure that the bird is sitting in a natural position and to check the position of the tail relative to the head. When you are satisfied, sand the underside to a fine finish. Mark in and drill the *himotoshi* as described in the dormouse project, starting on page 60.

Finishing

18 Once your carving is finished to your satisfaction, apply several coats of finishing oil. When each is dry, buff up to a shine. For alternative finishes see page 54.

RABBIT

This baby rabbit is a *Katabori* netsuke (see page 13) based on the same ovoid shape that was used for the turtle dove. The difficulty with this particular type of netsuke is that you need to carve all aspects of the subject, including the underside of the feet. Alternatively, place the subject on something else, such as a leaf or a log, so that the soles of the feet are hidden. In this case, I chose a cabbage leaf.

RABBIT

Toolbox

You will need the following:

Full-sized gouges:

1/4in (6mm) or 5/16in (8mm) number 3
1/4in (6mm) number 9

Palm tools or block cutters:

1/16in (1.5mm) number 39 V tool
1/16in (1.5mm) number 3
1/16in (1.5mm) veiner
1/32in (0.8mm) V tool (if possible)
1/8in (3mm) number 3
3/16in (4.5mm) number 3 or 4

Additional:

Plasticine
Small knife and/or scalpel
Abrasive grits 120–400
Magnifier – essential for carving fur
Acrylic paints and dyes

Materials

For this project, I chose my favourite timber for carving netsuke: boxwood. It is very hard, but takes fine detail, has a very attractive colour and much of it has good grain pattern. I prefer the home-grown variety, as it has a clarity and translucent quality not present in much of the imported wood.

You will need a piece about 3–4in (70–95mm) long and 1 3/4in (45mm) square, so that you have enough wood to hold while carving. When choosing the wood, avoid any pieces with evident end grain splits or those cut from small branches containing only heart wood, as these have a tendency to split.

Creating the maquette

The pictures below show the maquette from all sides, so you can make up patterns from any angle.

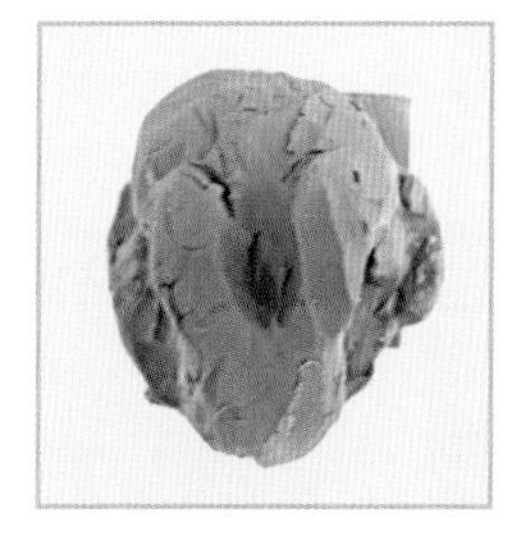

When making the maquette, remember that you need to leave enough wood for the cabbage leaf underneath the rabbit. Do not add detail to the leaf at this stage, you can come back to it after you have carved the baby rabbit.

If you choose to carve one of the many other types of rabbit, you may need to alter some of the details. For example, the ears can be larger, or the fur can be longer, carved or not carved. I have chosen a baby rabbit not an adult, therefore the anatomy is different. If you change this, check your proportions.

Design

We are going to include some additional techniques in this project, carving fur or hair and painting eyes. Full details of these can be found on pages 41 and 50. I recommend that you read these and that you take the time to practise on a spare piece of timber beforehand.

Producing the basic shape

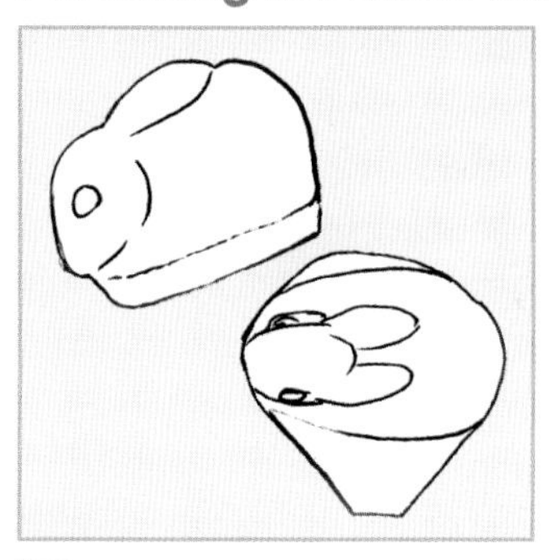

1 You will need to draw at least two patterns from your maquette, so that you can transfer the outlines to your block.

2 This carving will fit into the same basic shape that was used for the turtle dove, so the first thing to do is to repeat the early roughing out stages. However, this time, when you put the separation cuts between the carving and the support block, make sure that you leave enough space under the rabbit for the leaf. I suggest an extra ¼in (6mm) would be ample, making a total depth of about 2in (48mm) as shown on the right.

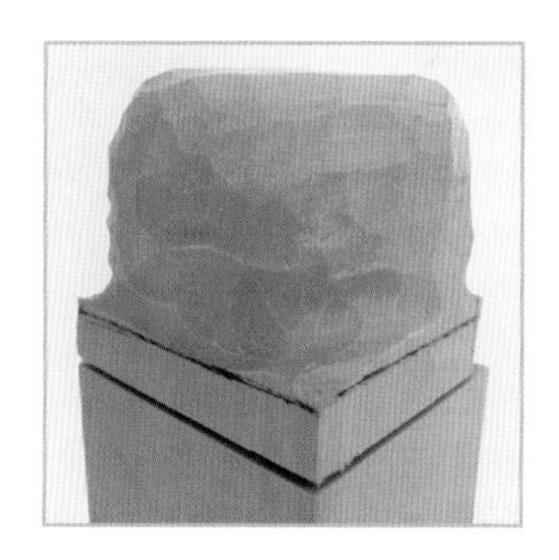

Setting out the figure

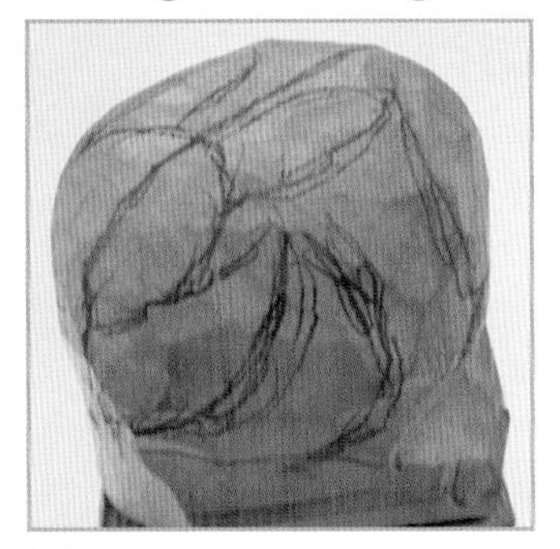

3 Using your patterns, draw the rough shape of the rabbit onto the oval shape you have created. Mark in the position of the ears.

TIP: You may find it useful to draw the patterns onto some clear acetate with a permanent pen. This way you can check where the various parts of the animal should be by holding the acetate over your carving.

Getting the limbs right

4 Rough out the shape you have drawn using a small gouge or veiner – keep the whole shape soft with no hard edges and do not undercut anywhere. Remember that the rabbit is sitting on a leaf, which will come out of the wood underneath the oval shape you have made.

5 Using the reference material, redefine the rough shape of the rabbit's limbs, making sure that the shape is the same on both sides. It is not critical that the legs are exactly the right length, yet it is important that each pair of legs are symmetrical. The rabbit has thick fur, so do not define the legs too much. Although bear in mind that when carving a piece of this size, a small error of measurement can make a dramatic difference.

6 Check the size of the head in relation to the rest of the rabbit's body, using photographs or real-life examples for comparison. It is very easy to get this wrong and, as a result, end up with a small adult rabbit instead of a baby one. Also, ensure that the position of the eyes and ears are correct. Make a note of these for later.

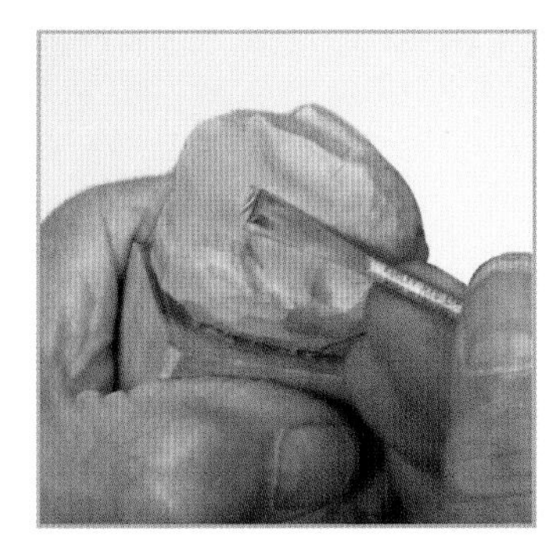

7 Continue the roughing out, refining and checking the structure as you go along. It does not matter whether you follow the shape shown here, but try to keep the 'feel' of a baby rabbit. A small number 3 or 4 fishtail is very useful for this.

8 Cut the carving off its base. Although this will make it slightly more difficult to hold, it will give you much better access to those awkward little corners.

Shaping the head

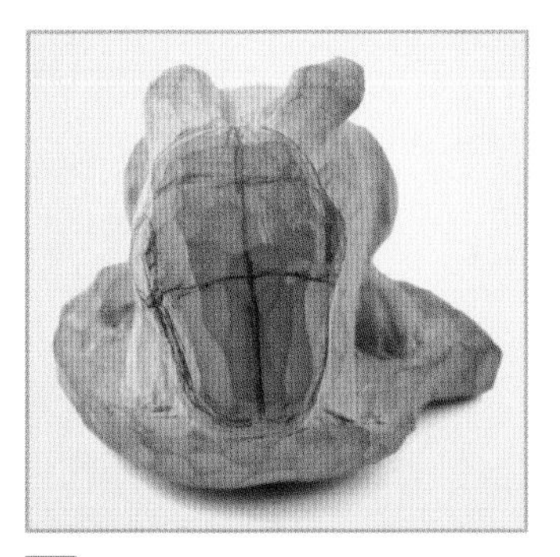

9 You can now start to add details to the head. You do not want to detract from the soft shape you have created, so ensure that you keep the ears close to the body.

10 Make sure that you leave some wood between the nose and the base, as the cabbage leaf has to meet the mouth. Leave plenty more wood for the bulge of the eyes and under the eyes, as the cheeks on a baby rabbit are quite prominent - draw these in at this stage.

TIP: The order in which you follow the steps is not important. If you wish to carve the eyes before adding texture to the fur, go ahead. I prefer to add the fur first to avoid any damage to the eyes.

11 Spend some time making sure that you have created the shape you were aiming for. It is important not to rush this stage, for once you have carved the fur any changes will mean having to carve the whole piece again.

12 Now, start to shape the cabbage leaf. Curl up the part of the leaf under the head, as this has to meet the rabbit's mouth. The top surface can be cleaned as you cut around the feet.

13 When you are happy with the rabbit's shape, you can begin to carve the detail on the ears. Keep the ears resting on the back of the rabbit and do not make them too thin.

Smoothing off

14 When satisfied, give the whole piece a good sanding. The next step is to carve the fur, if you decide you want to add this feature. Concentrate on getting rid of as many pencil marks as possible, as you will not be able to do this once you have finished.

Carving the fur

When considering whether to add fur to your subject or not, you need to weigh up whether it will improve the carving. If you are in any doubt, leave it. Netsuke pieces are frequently spoilt by over carving. If you decide to go ahead, take care not to overdo it.

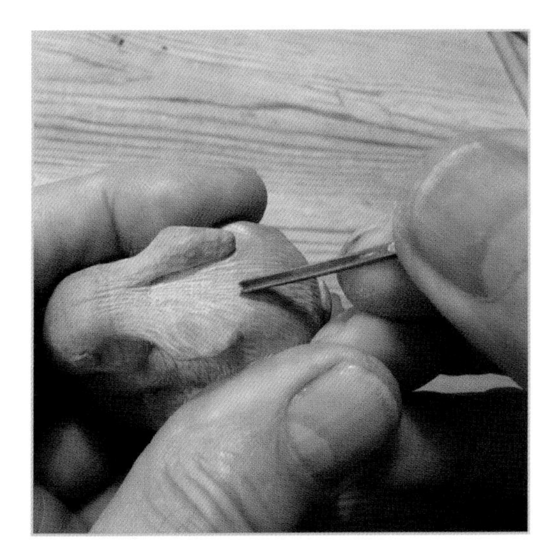

15 To do this you will need a very fine cut. Your V tool will therefore need to be extremely sharp and capable of cutting a very fine line. You may wish to get a smaller tool, around 1/32in (0.7mm), or use a fine rotary burr in a power tool. You could even try burning the texture using a pyrography tool.

NB: Check that you know in which direction the fur lies on the body. With your small veiner tool go over the surface very lightly in the direction of the lie of the fur until you have a faint texture all over.

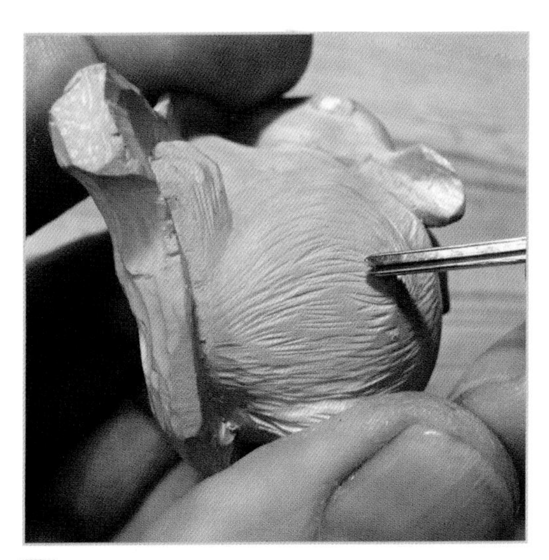

16 Either leave it there or repeat the texturing process using your fine V tool, going over what you have already done. This process can be done as many times as you like, until you have achieved the desired effect.

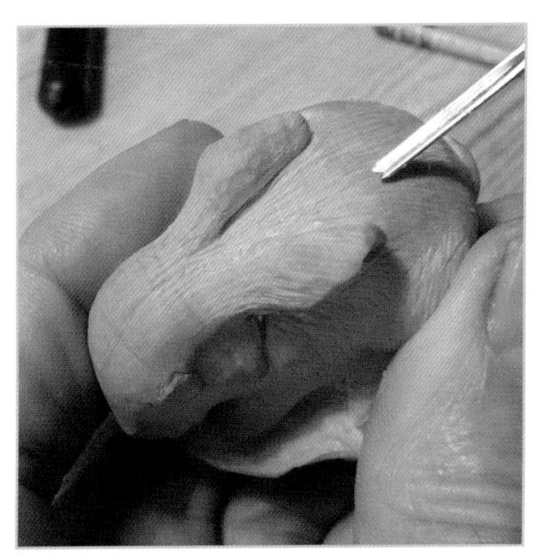

17 Make sure that you do all this very lightly, taking off tiny pieces of wood each time. Keep the strokes short and try to make each one a very shallow 'S' in shape. It is a good idea to go all over the rabbit every time to ensure that the texture is consistently applied. To obtain a good effect, your tools need to be extremely sharp and may need touching up several times during the process.

Carving the eyes

The rabbit's eye is carved before being painted. If you are feeling confident, you could inlay a separate eye. This is covered in a later project, but if you wish to try it now refer to the section on carving eyes on page 40.

18 The following applies to the carving of most animal eyes. Firstly, you may find it is useful to wear a pair of disposable gloves to keep the piece clean. Secondly, the eyes should be carved as if they were closed, so in fact you are producing the eyeball, not the open eye. The open eye will be carved later.

19 Rabbits are prey animals and grazers, therefore they need to be able to see both sides and the rear. For that reason, carefully locate the position of the eyes on each side of the head, making sure that there is a clear line of sight through almost 180 degrees. Checking from the top and the front, confirm that both eyes are symmetrically placed. Then, mark the circle lightly with a pencil and carve the mound of the eye. Keep checking that both sides remain the same.

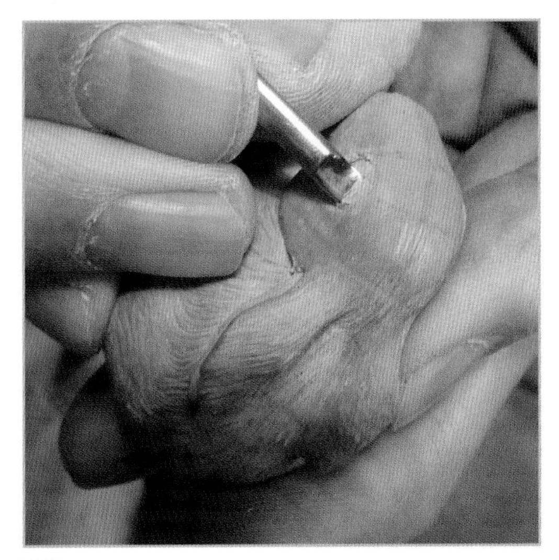

20 Draw the outline of each eye on the mound, again confirming that they are symmetrical. On larger eyes a pattern is useful to ensure that both sides are equal. Carefully cut around the top, then the bottom edge of each eye. Do not stray from the lines you have drawn so carefully.

21 Round the inside of the eye into these cuts, while maintaining the spherical shape of the eyeball. Take your time, it is very easy to end up with an almond shape if you are not careful. Finally, check that both eyes look the same.

Detailing the leaf

22 Before starting to carve the leaf, obtain a cabbage leaf for reference. Study the surface detail. You do not need to reproduce it exactly, but it does need to be recognizable. The underside of the leaf can now be shaped. Curl the edges to strengthen them and to make them feel smoother.

Adding the himotoshi

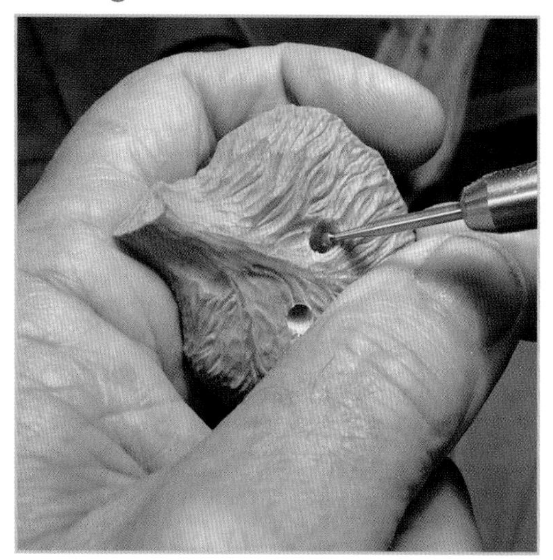

23 It is not important exactly where on the underneath you place the *himotoshi*. Repeat the process detailed on page 68, making sure that the holes are both clean and smooth.

Painting the eyes

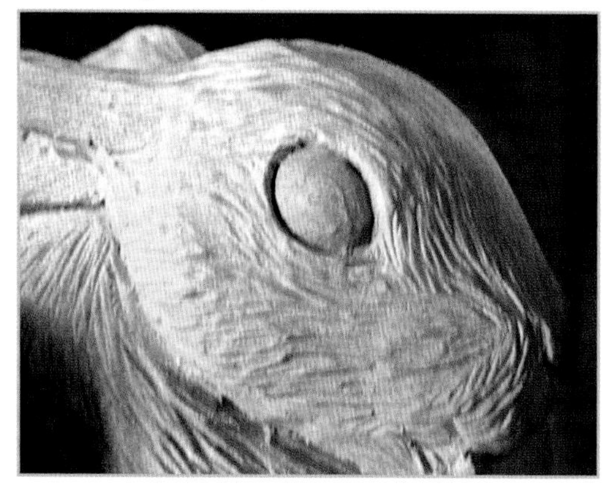

24 Before adding paint to the eyes, ensure that the surface of the eyeball is completely smooth and clean. Sand it down with the finest abrasive you can find, then wipe off any trace of dust. Coat the eye with a universal sealer and allow to dry. This is readily available from hobby shops. Next, add a coat of yellow acrylic watercolour to brighten the finish.

25 Add a coat of dark brown to the whole eye, before colouring the pupil black. The eye looks more natural if you darken the top of the eye slightly. To finish, a drop of clear nail varnish in each eye will provide the necessary sparkle. Sometimes two very small white spots can add to this effect.

TIP: Use a toothpick or something similar to collect a drop of varnish. Holding the surface of the eye flat, let this drop onto the eye. Do not brush it on as this may leave brush marks.

Finishing

I have chosen to add colour to this piece using a Procion fabric dye. The advantage of this over many other fabric dyes is that it does not need to be used hot. It is also very powerful, so you only need the tiniest spot mixed with water.

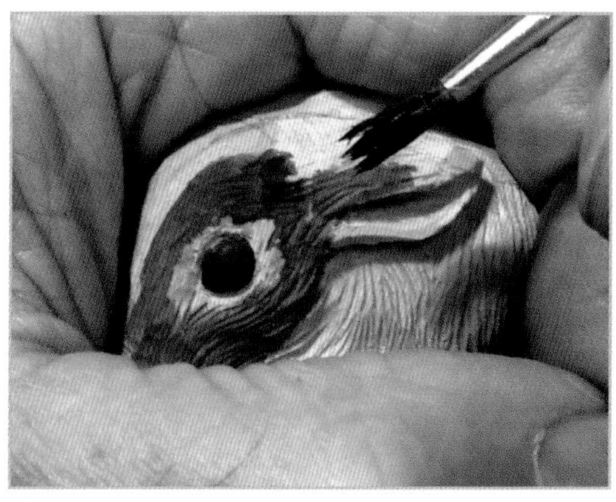

26 Brush the fabric dye onto the piece with a fine brush, taking care not to spill over onto the cabbage leaf. Shade around the eyes, nose and inside the ears, leaving these areas lighter.

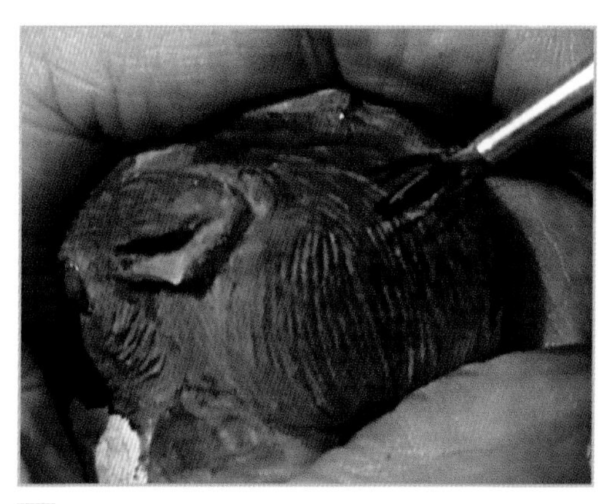

27 You can experiment with the colour as you wish to make it even or shaded. Once you are satisfied with the colour, give the whole carving a coat of finishing oil or wax if you prefer.

TIP: There are many options when it comes to colours. Experiment with the various options with some waste material before applying it to your carving, to avoid mistakes. Be cautious with wood stains as they tend to go much darker on areas of end grain.

FISH

Fish are one of the most common subjects used for netsuke carvings as they feature strongly in Japanese history and culture,as well as being a sign of the zodiac. Fish are also ideal for simple design exercises, for they can be used to explore techniques such as carving scales or inlaying eyes without worrying too much about carving the details or anatomy correctly.

FISH

Toolbox

You will need the following:

Full-sized gouges:

1/4in (6mm) number 3
1/4in (6mm) number 3

Palm gouges or block cutters:

1/8in (3mm) number 9
1/16in (1.5mm) number 1 chisel
3/16in (4.5mm) number 2 skew chisel
1/8in (3mm) number 3
1/16in (1.5mm) number 39 V tool

Additional:

Plasticine
Electric drill and 1/8in (3mm) bit
Amber for the eyes

Materials

For this project I chose a piece of yew, as it produces fantastic grain patterns. Yew is one of the few timbers that often works much better when green or 'undried', especially as it has a tendency to split when dry. This particular piece had some very small splits in it, however I decided to use it regardless, simply to see how it would turn out. In many cases applying oil as you carve causes these faults to disappear. You could, of course, use your own preferred timber.

Creating the maquette

The pictures below show the maquette from all sides, so you can make up patterns from any angle.

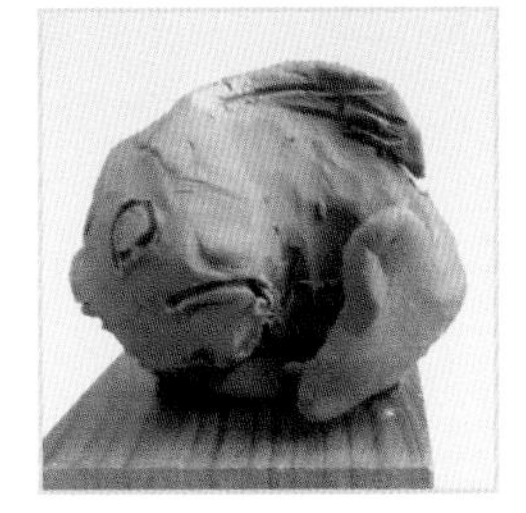

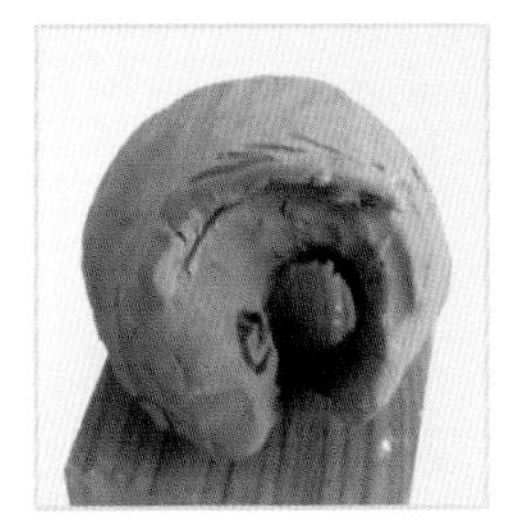

The maquette in this project is only an indication of the shape of the fish. You will find that you add your own personal touches as you go along.

Producing the basic shape

1 The fish is another subject which is based on a ball or a sphere. You can carve it in the same way as the dormouse, (starting on page 60) or turn it on a lathe. The shape follows the curves of the ball; vary these as you wish.

2 The faults in my piece of yew wood dictated the shape I chose. I was forced to modify the maquette to avoid these faults, ultimately reversing my design. This demonstrates the need to be flexible, particularly during the design stage.

3 Fish come in so many varied shapes that it is hard to get the shape wrong. They can be thin, fat, long or short. Create a simple outline, letting the lines flow and ensuring that the parts do not stick out.

4 Do not forget to leave enough wood for the fins. Refer to photographs to make sure that you get the right number of fins positioned correctly. Keep them as close to the body as possible.

5 When you are happy with the shape, sand it smooth.

Carving the scales

You will find it very difficult to carve the scales as they actually appear. Even expert netsuke carvers never claim to have carved accurate representations of their subjects, simply the 'jizz' of the animal. Therefore, show the scales in any way you deem effective. For further details refer to page 45.

6 Lay out the scale pattern on your carving before starting to cut them out. Fish scales lie in a diagonal pattern, so start by drawing a series of diagonal lines along the back of the fish.

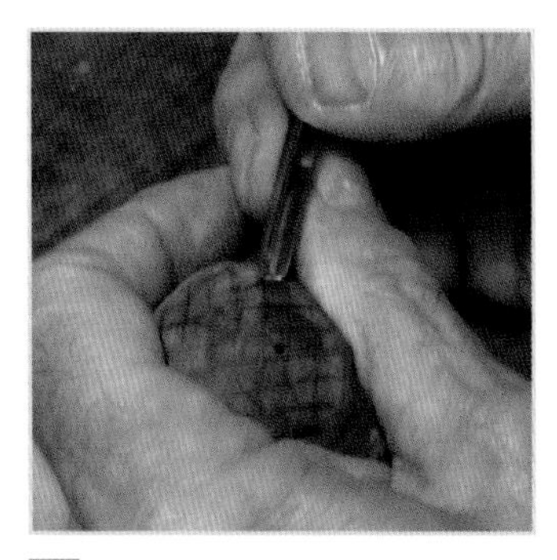

7 Cut these lines with a small V tool, around ⅛in (3mm) or a 1/16in (1.5mm) in size. One side of the V should rest on the timber, producing a slight undercut on one side and a smooth flat face on the other.

8 Make sure that the scales overlap in the right direction. Each scale should overlap the next one as you work towards the tail. This is a tedious process and will almost certainly require a magnifier. Take your time, particularly in the difficult to reach areas.

9 When you have finished, clean out all the corners with a scalpel or small skew chisel, before giving the whole thing a good sanding. If you have used a hard wood, you can afford to be quite vigorous as the scales should not be dominant. Any scales that are accidently flattened can be recut if necessary.

10 Next, mark out and carve the inside scales. This is a lot more difficult and will require a large amount of experimentation to perfect.

11 Any final detailing of the fins and the tail can now be added using your V tool.

Making the eyes

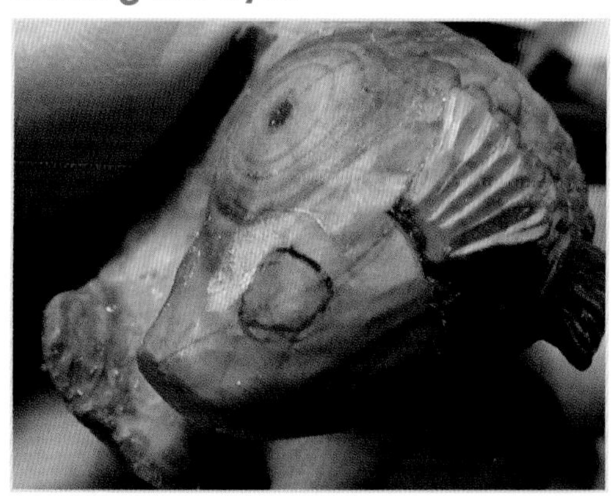

12 If you are going to inlay the eyes, roughly carve them first to ensure that they are in the correct position. Then flatten them and draw the exact locations ready for drilling. Once you have drilled the holes you cannot go back, so check their position thoroughly.

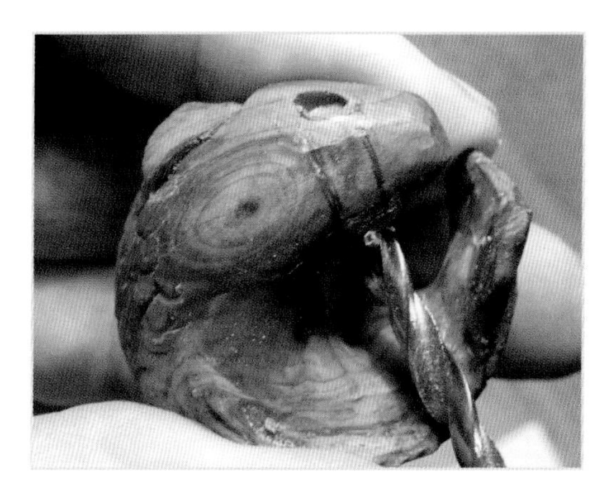

13 Decide how large the eyes will be and drill the appropriately sized holes on each side of the head. I used a 5⁄32in (4mm) woodbit with a central point so that it did not slip while I was drilling the holes.

14 To fit the eye, drill another hole of the same size in a spare piece of yew. Do not use the hole in your carving for the fitting as you could get the eye stuck or damage the socket.

TIP: I used amber for the eyes, but there are many other materials that you could use if you prefer.

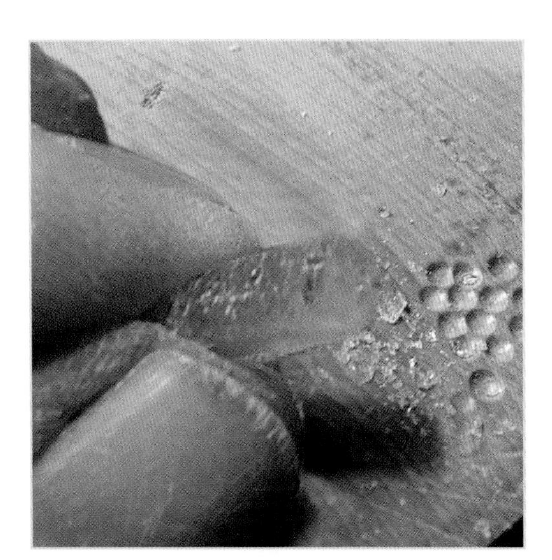

15 Cut a length of amber with a junior hacksaw, then scrape it to shape using a scalpel. Power tools are not suitable for use with amber, as it is natural resin and may therefore melt with heat.

16 Fit the dowel into the fitting hole of the spare piece of yew. Then make a small hollow in one end with the end of a $^{1}/_{16}$in (1.5mm) drill bit or round-headed dental burr.

17 Paint this black to represent the pupil of the eye. This is not easy to do while holding the amber in your fingertips. Instead, hold it in a pin vice, although be aware that amber is very brittle and tends to break easily.

TIP: You may find it easier to fit the amber eye first, then drill a hole right through the middle. You can then insert a very thin dowel of ebony or buffalo horn for the pupil. You will need to use extra small drill bits to do this. The sort used for printed circuit boards are ideal and can usually be obtained from electronic suppliers.

Fitting the eyes

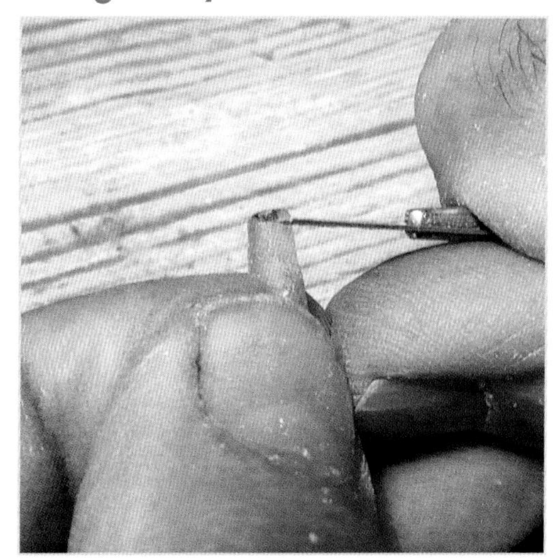

18 Check that the eyes will fit into the socket on your carving. Any adjustments to the shape are best done by scraping with your scalpel.

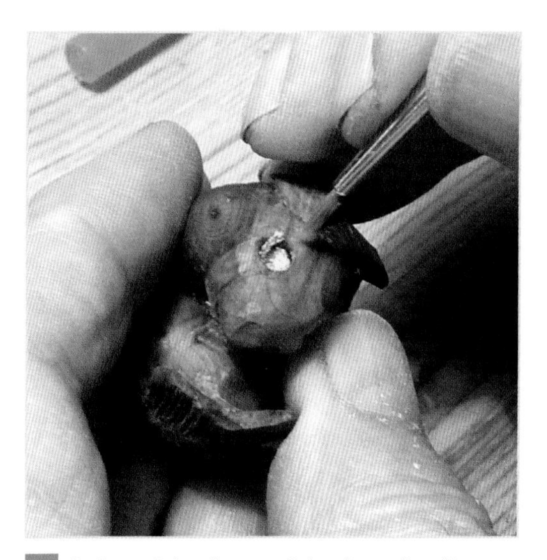

19 Before gluing the eye into place, line the socket with gold-leaf paper – toffee wrappers are excellent for this job.

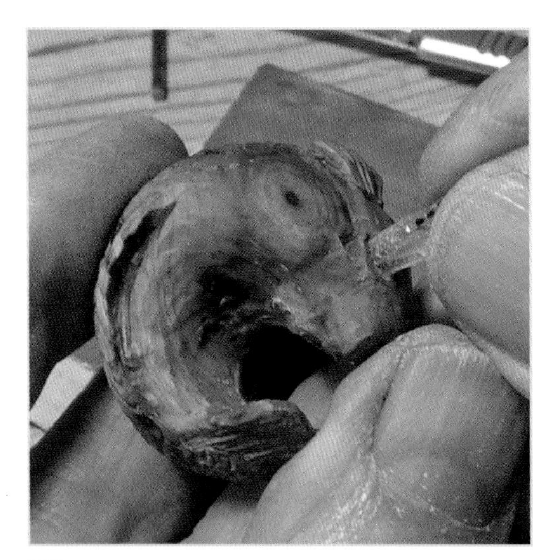

20 Cut part of the way through the eye stick you have made and glue into place using high-strength adhesive.

21 When it is set, trim off any surplus material and polish with a fine abrasive, such as 1500 grit, before finishing off with 1200 grit. More details of this process can be found on page 42.

Finishing

TIP: When using amber for the eyes, it is very likely that the resin dust will begin to build up around the edge. Leave this until you have oiled the whole piece. Should it still be obvious, careful polishing should remove it or, if necessary, add a small amount of clear varnish.

22 If you have used yew wood, you may well find imperfections in the wood. In my opinion these simply add to its charm.

Finishing

TIP: The advantage of yew over many other timbers is its wonderful colour and grain patterns. However, it also has a marked tendency to split, especially when dry. I therefore recommend that you finish this piece with a finishing oil, preferably one that does not dry too quickly, such as boiled or raw linseed or olive oil.

23 Let the finishing oil dry over a period of a week, then finish off with Danish oil, which will go over any other finish. If you rub this in with your fingers you will get a nice patina to the piece. Although remember to wash any surplus off your hands before it dries.

WARNING: If you have used oil during the carving process, avoid using teak oil as this could react with other finishes. It should really only be used on bare wood or wood that has already had teak oil on it.

TOAD

This carving is fun to make and with so many variations almost impossible to get wrong, so long as the basic structure is adhered to. The toad is also an ideal subject to use to introduce three new techniques. In order to concentrate on these techniques, I have kept to a very simple design, leaving you room to be as ambitious as you want.

TOAD

Toolbox

You will need the following:

Palm tools or block cutters:

1/8in (3mm) number 1 or 2 chisel
1/8in (3mm) number 3
1/16in (1.5mm) number 39 V tool
1/4in (6mm) number 3 gouge
1/4in (6mm) number 9 gouge
1/16in (1.5mm) number 9 or 11 veiner
3/16in (4.5mm) number 2 skew chisel
3/16in (4.5mm) number 9 gouge

Full-sized gouges:

1/4in (6mm) number 3 gouge (fish-tail or straight)
1/4in (6mm) number 9 gouge (fish-tail or straight)

Additional:

Plasticine
A round-ended punch
A drill and drill bits
Some high-strength adhesive
(and perhaps a hot melt glue gun)
Abrasive
Electric multi-tool
Amber or similar, buffalo horn and plastic beads
for the eyes
Ram's horn for the *himotoshi*

Materials

Apple wood is readily obtained, as well as being a very inexpensive alternative to some of the more exotic and costly timbers. It is simple to carve, takes fine detail and finishes well. Apple can be very hard, particularly when kiln-dried, but it can be used green or 'undried' if you prefer. This will mean having to work slightly differently. There are some guidelines to make this easier on page 20.

Creating the maquette

The pictures below show the maquette from all sides, so you can make up patterns from any angle.

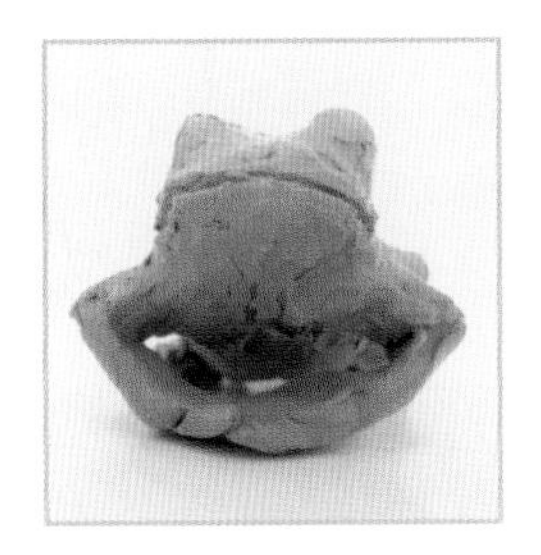

Look carefully at a range of photographs, paying particular attention to the shape of a toad's back legs, as many carvers get these wrong. Take note of where and how the front legs attach to the body. Modify the general shape of the toad, primarily the front and back toes, so that it fits the requirements of a netsuke. In general, frogs have webbed feet whereas toads do not. However, if a toad's feet are carved as they occur naturally, they would break off either during the carving process or soon afterwards. Therefore, we need to shorten and thicken the feet slightly to make them stronger.

Producing the basic shape

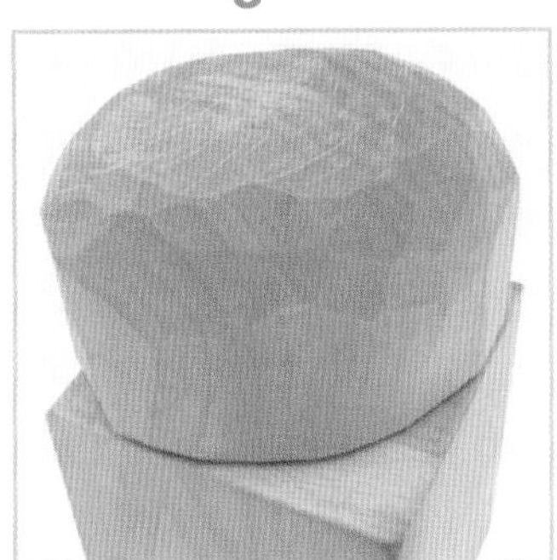

1 Rough out the block into an ovoid shape.

2 Draw the side outline using the patterns drawn from the maquette to obtain the right pose. Cut away the waste straight across the block with no rounding off at all.

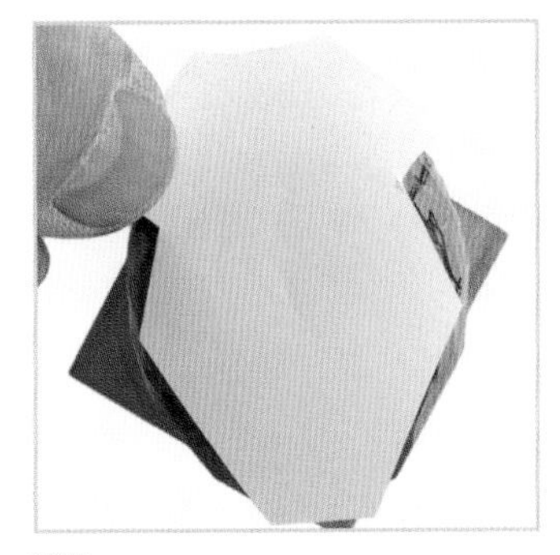

3 You may find it useful to make a card pattern of the top view, so as to make your block look more 'toad shaped'. Draw this on the top of your block.

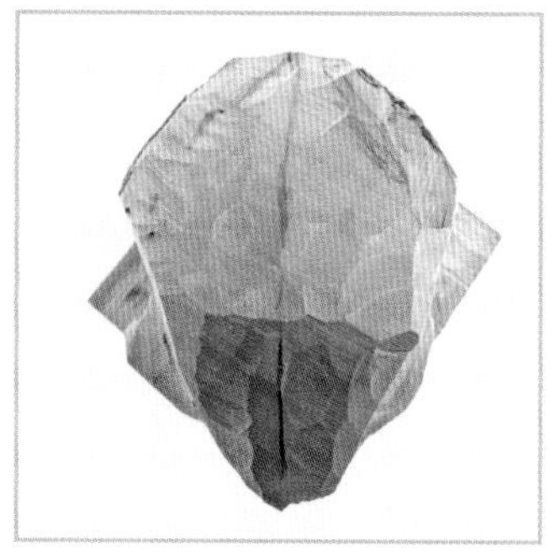

4 Cut away the waste from this view. This should leave you with a square toad shape, yet without any discernible legs.

5 Next, lower the front section to around half the height to define the area within which the front legs will be situated.

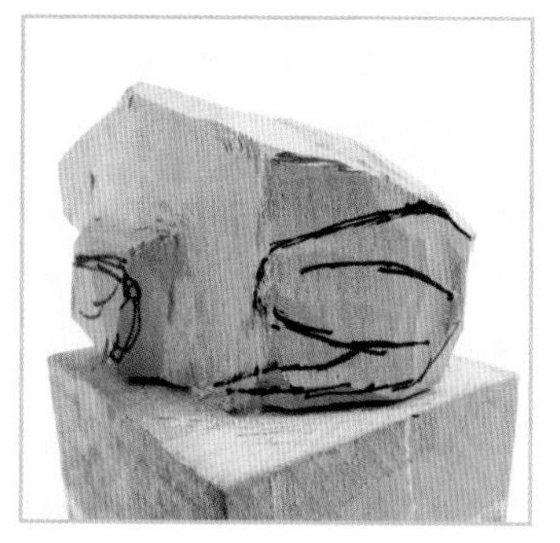

6 Mark in the back legs. These will look more realistic if the knees are carved lower than the hips.

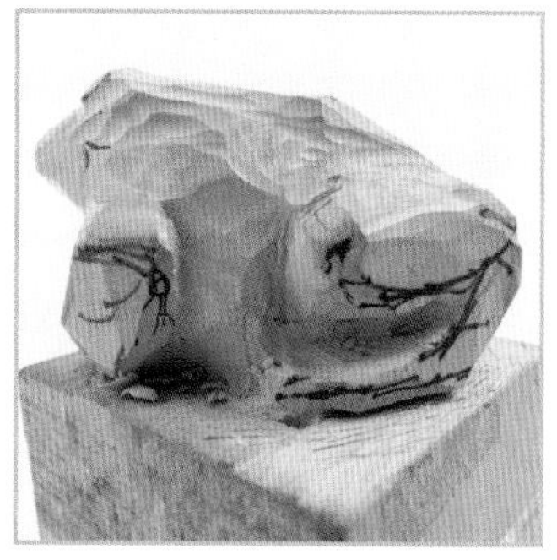

7 Remove the waste above and below, before starting to round off the back of both front legs.

8 Start to shape your toad, rounding off the legs and shaping the body. Keep the whole piece quite chunky; you can always fine it down later. Check your maquette and reference material regularly to ensure that you are carving the shape correctly.

9 Cut between the front legs to get the shape of the chest right. Be careful not to break the feet as they have very short grain. Also, sort out the rough shape of the feet, bearing in mind that keeping them fairly heavy at this stage is advisable.

10 I suggest sanding the toad at this stage to check its overall shape. Some people are of the opinion that you should not sand your netsuke if you are going to continue carving, as the sand particles may damage the edge of your tools. However, as long as you wipe your carving off afterwards, this should not cause any problems. Choose an abrasive that does not clog or leave any obvious residue, such as cellular abrasives.

Ukibori

There is always the possibility that you will spoil your carving when adding further details. For this reason, add the bumps before fitting the eyes or the *himotoshi*. As the bumps will only be on the back and sides, they should not affect the rest of your work. As results vary considerably from one timber to another, I recommend experimenting on a spare piece of apple wood before moving on to your carving. Remember that the majority of the bumps will be on the back, which is end grain, so make sure that you practise on end grain. The *ukibori* is described in detail on page 51, so I will be brief here.

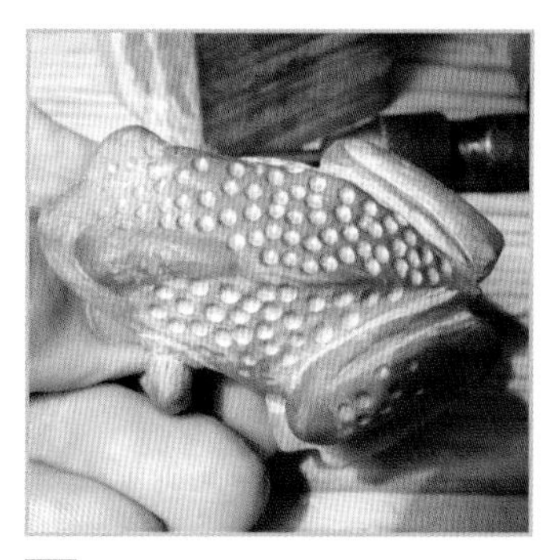

11 Using a smooth, round-ended punch, make a series of dents along the back and the sides of your carving. If you are using an automatic centre punch, you can vary the depth to suit or 'fade' the bumps at the edges by making them smaller in size.

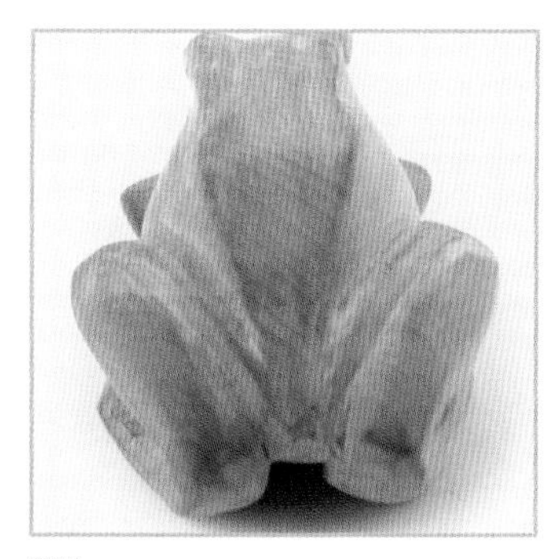

12 Sand the wood around these dents until the whole surface is smooth. You should still be able to see where you have made the dents. Be careful not to sand down too far or you will not achieve the desired texture.

TIP: In real life, the warts on a toad tend to be very close together. This cannot be easily reproduced on the netsuke as there is a danger that the fibres between the dents will break. I strongly recommend therefore that you practise on a spare piece of the same wood and use whatever density you find successful.

13 Once you are happy that the surface is uniformly smooth, wet it all over with warm water. You will immediately notice that the dents rise into bumps on the surface. Leave it to dry out thoroughly.

14 You may find that giving the surface a finishing coat adds to the piece. Use Danish oil or something similar, as this will help to keep the surface clean. Do not sand it down again afterwards.

TIP: If there are areas where the bumps did not come out exactly as you wanted, do not worry. Simply repeat the process, taking care not to sand off the bumps that you want to keep.

Making and fitting the eyes

Carve the eyes next, as this will involve some fiddling with the shape of the head before adding the fine details. This is covered in more detail on page 43, so we will only cover the basics here.

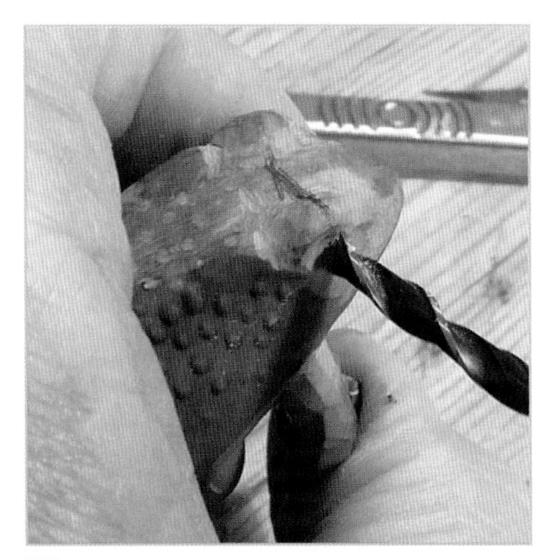

15 First, draw a line across the top of the toad's head to mark the position of the eyes. Then drill out the sockets. You will need to flatten the mound you have carved. Use a 100in (5mm) wood bit with a centre point to drill the holes.

16 Take care to ensure that the holes on each side line up exactly. Use the line that you drew across the top of the head as a guide.

17 It is a good idea to drill a hole the same size in a spare piece of apple wood for the early fitting. Try the material carefully in the eye socket to get the final shape. Be careful not to push too hard in the hole.

18 I used an amber substitute for the eyes, as it is a lot easier to work with. The best source for this is beads, especially those that are translucent and brightly coloured. Check that the beads will polish to a good shine beforehand; it would be a shame to go to the trouble of making the eyes, only to find that they finish up dull.

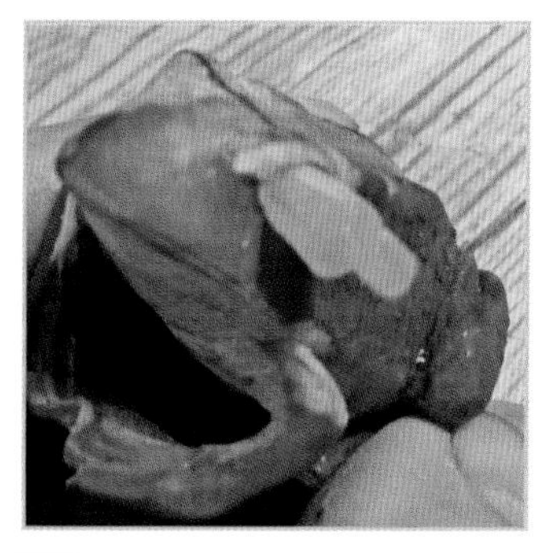

19 Cut the material with a small saw, such as a mini hacksaw, then file or sand it into a thin cylinder shape. Alternatively, hold it in a rotary multi-tool and spin it on some cloth-backed abrasive, but watch the dust. The material will need to be a little larger than the hole you have drilled in the head.

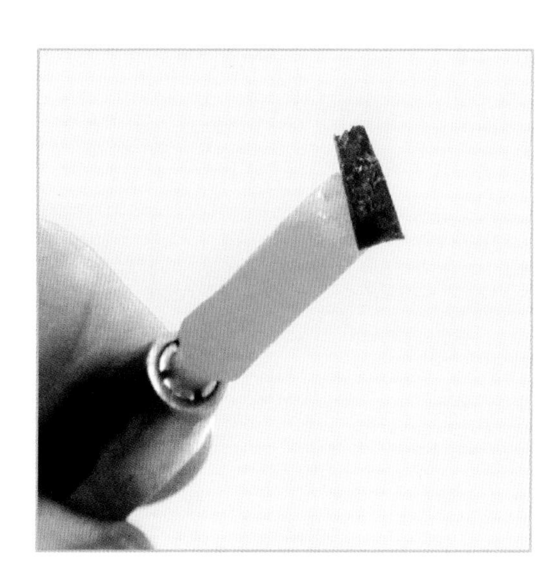

20 Next, cut a 90-degree groove in the end using a square-section needle file. Cut a piece of buffalo horn to fit the groove and fix it firmly in place using a high-strength adhesive. A small pin vice is a useful tool to hold the eye while you file and polish it. Fit the eye gently into the socket you have carved. Do not push it too hard or you could damage the socket or even break the eye.

NB: See the section on eyes on page 43 for the complete process.

TIP: The next step can be quite tricky, as you need to cut the eye to size before fitting it. As the eye is so small, it is very difficult to handle. One solution is to cut an old ball-pen case to size and cut two slits in the sides to hold the eye securely. If this is not firm enough for the final fitting, fill the end with hot melt glue to hold the eye firmly.

21 Mark the direction of the pupil on the bottom of the eye before gluing it to ensure that both eyes line up.

22 Fitting the eyes is simply a matter of trial and error. Sand each eye down slowly until it fits, then glue it securely into place. I have used a backing of gold leaf for an added sparkle – gold toffee paper does the job equally well – fixed into place with putty or epoxy glue.

Final details

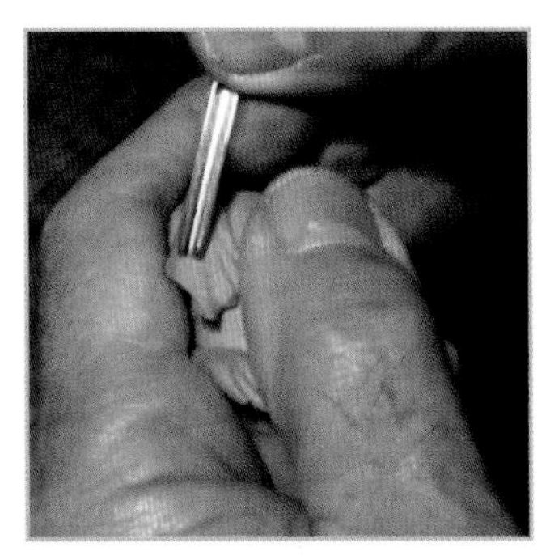

23 Before carving the front and back feet, make sure that you know exactly how many toes there are on each foot. Remember that you need to carve both the top and the underneath of the netsuke.

24 Draw the mouth carefully, ensuring that it is even on both sides, particularly from the front. When you are satisfied, cut it carefully with a small V tool, then round off the edges with a needle file and fine abrasive.

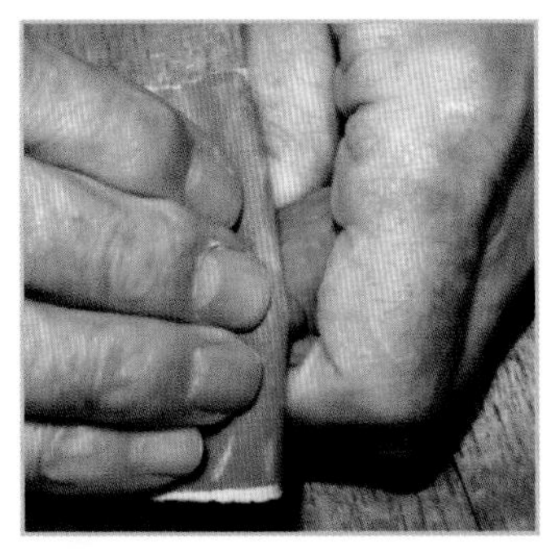

25 Finally, sand the whole piece, being careful to watch out for the bumps.

Adding the himotoshi

26 The easiest and quickest way to add the *himotoshi* is shown in the previous projects (see page 68). However, if you decide you want to be a bit more adventurous you could add some inlay. I have added two inlays of ram's horn as outlined in detail on page 56. These pictures show the simple *himotoshi* (left), alongside the inlaid one (right).

Finishing

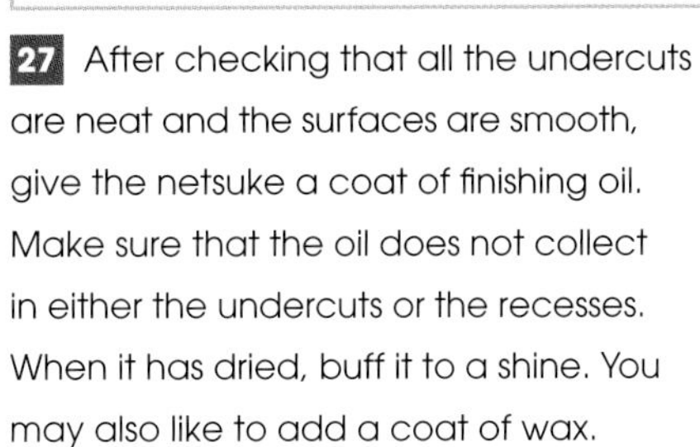

27 After checking that all the undercuts are neat and the surfaces are smooth, give the netsuke a coat of finishing oil. Make sure that the oil does not collect in either the undercuts or the recesses. When it has dried, buff it to a shine. You may also like to add a coat of wax.

MONKEY

The monkey on the pot is designed to show two subjects interacting in the one carving. It is this interaction that really brings the carving to life. Monkeys are similar to small children in that they cannot resist putting their hands into small objects or holes, often getting themselves into trouble. The monkey has been searching for something inside the pot, but all he has found is his tail. He has not got the sense to let it go and to pull his hand out.

MONKEY

Toolbox

You will need the following:

Full-sized gouges:

$^{1}/_{4}$in (6mm) number 3 gouge (fish-tail or straight)
$^{1}/_{4}$in (6mm) number 9 gouge (fish-tail or straight)

Palm tools or block cutters:

$^{1}/_{8}$in (3mm) number 1 or 2 chisel
$^{1}/_{8}$in (3mm) number 3
$^{1}/_{16}$in (1.5mm) number 39 V tool or smaller
$^{1}/_{4}$in (6mm) number 3 gouge
$^{1}/_{4}$in (6mm) number 9 gouge
$^{1}/_{16}$in (1.5mm) number 9 or 11 veiner
$^{3}/_{16}$in (4.5mm) number 2 skew chisel
$^{3}/_{16}$in (4.5mm) number 9 gouge

Additional:

Plasticine
Home-made small scrapers and chisels
Abrasive
Small files or rifflers
Buffalo horn for the eyes

Materials

For this piece I went back to my personal favourite, boxwood, but you can use an alternative wood if you prefer.

NB: Power tools are not recommended for this project, as you will have problems getting them in deep enough. You can, of course, modify the design to suit the tools you have available.

Creating the maquette

The monkey I have carved is based on the fairly similar squirrel or spider monkeys. There is plenty of reference material available on these animals to ensure that the details are correct.

Make a plasticine model of the pot, then fit a rough monkey shape on top, identifying where each part should be. It is important to create the pot first, as it has a definite shape that is important to get right. The monkey can be arranged to suit, to a certain extent.

TIP: Use the maquette to check that you can get your tools into all the odd corners and recesses in your design. I found it difficult to get right to the bottom of the pot, so I had to create an alternative access point, hence the hole in the side – it could easily be a broken pot. Now we have a story and a touch of humour.

Producing the basic shape

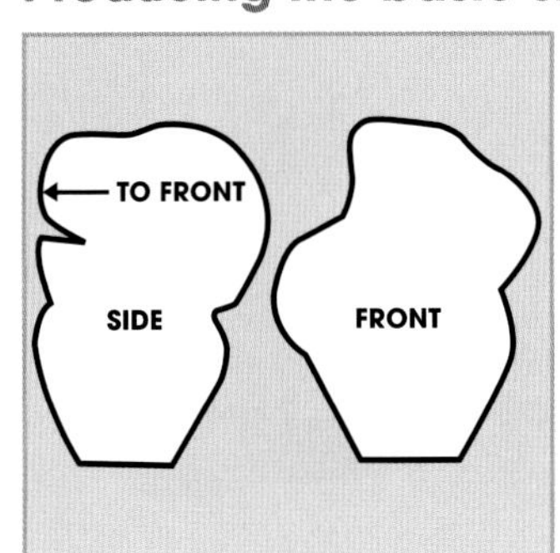

1 Draw a pattern using the maquette as a template.

2 Draw around the outline to produce the shape of the timber you will need. Ensure that you leave enough wood all around for both the monkey and the pot. Then cut out the shape using either a bandsaw or a coping saw.

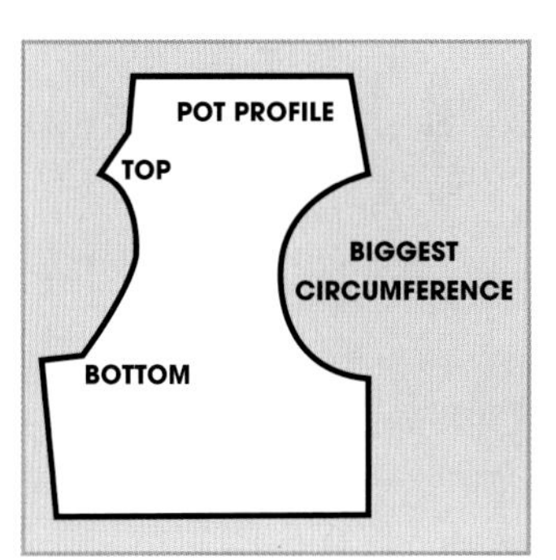

3 When you are happy with the overall design, start to round off the pot. It is important to get the curves right, so make a card pattern for both the top and sides profiles. These can be used to check the shape of your netsuke as you progress.

Rounding off

4 Round off the pot using a knife or a small number 9 gouge. Do not worry if the pot is not completely round at this stage. There will be plenty of time to adjust it later on. There is also a strong possibility that you will damage the pot while carving the detail of the monkey. The whole process will involve adjusting and modifying as the need arises.

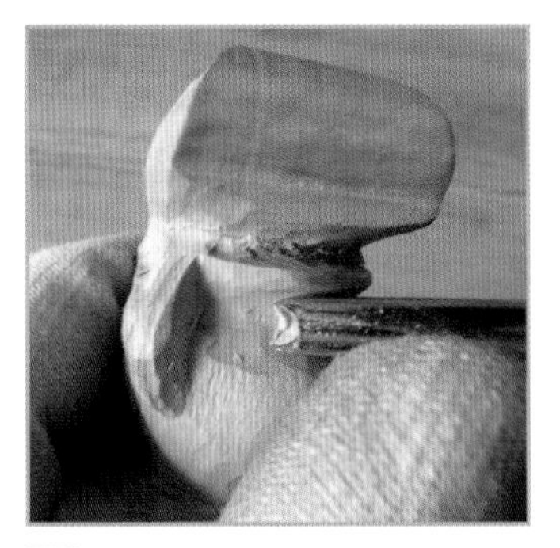

5 Continue until you are satisfied with the shape, before evenly sanding your carving. Do not be tempted to remove too much wood from the inside of the pot until the monkey is roughed out.

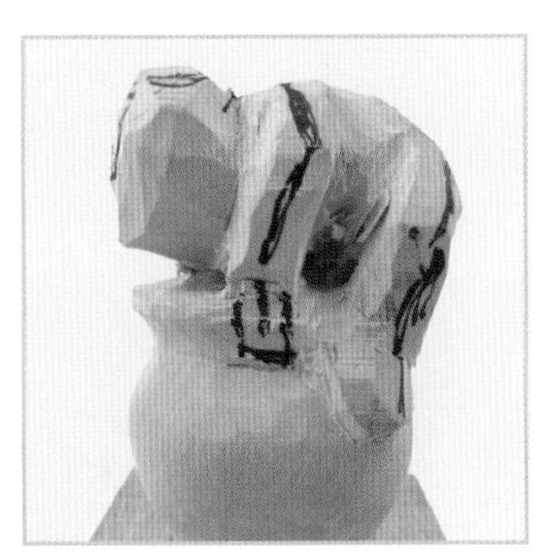

6 Moving onto the monkey, refer to the maquette for the position of its legs and hands. Do not stray too far from this or you will find that you cannot access the inside of the pot. Check that the limbs on both sides are of equal lengths. To help, you could make up some wire guides as shown on page 65.

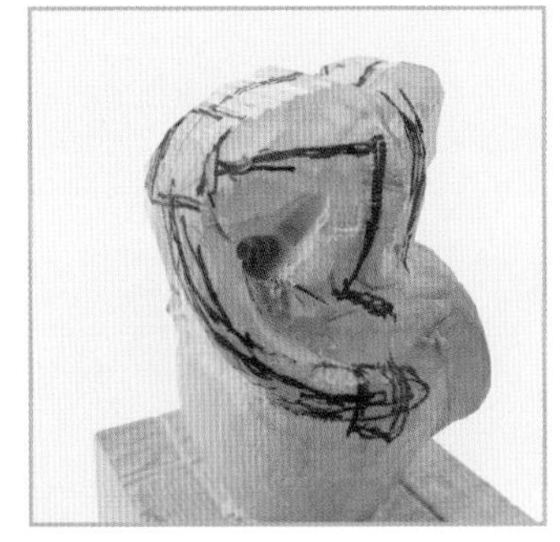

7 Do not take the limbs down too fine at this stage. There is still quite a lot of work to do in order to hollow out the pot and you do not want to break off any of the limbs that you have carved.

8 Any refining of the overall shape or extra sanding should be done at this stage. You should also drill the hole in the side of the pot while you have something to hold on to.

Cut off the base

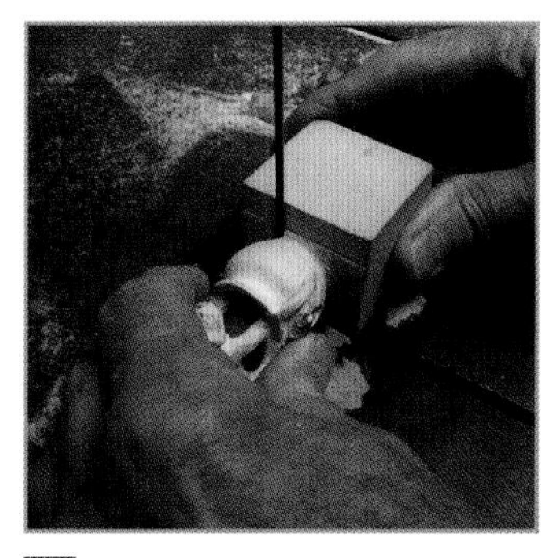

9 Cut off the carving using a bandsaw or a coping saw. This will make it difficult to hold, but also more manoeuvrable for getting into all the little nooks and crannies.

10 Now it is off the base, check that the bottom of the pot is circular. If it is not, sand it down. Use your template to check the overall shape.

TIP: The hole in the side of the pot was added primarily to gain access to the inside of the pot. The shape can be altered as required to make it easier to get the tools where you need them.

Hollowing the pot

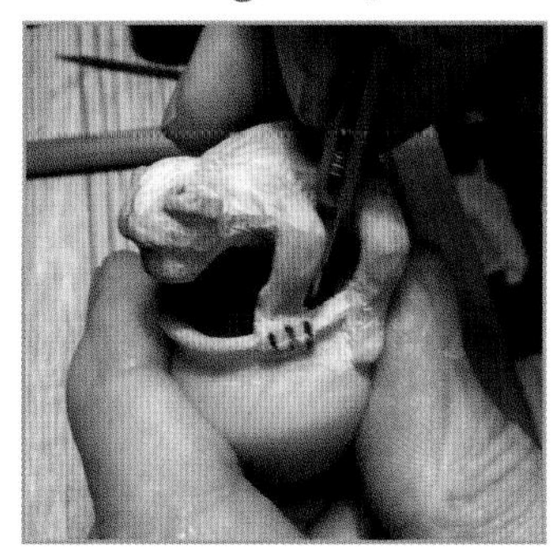

11 There is no correct tool to use for hollowing out the pot; simply use whichever tool does the job. All that is necessary is to obtain a reasonably smooth interior.

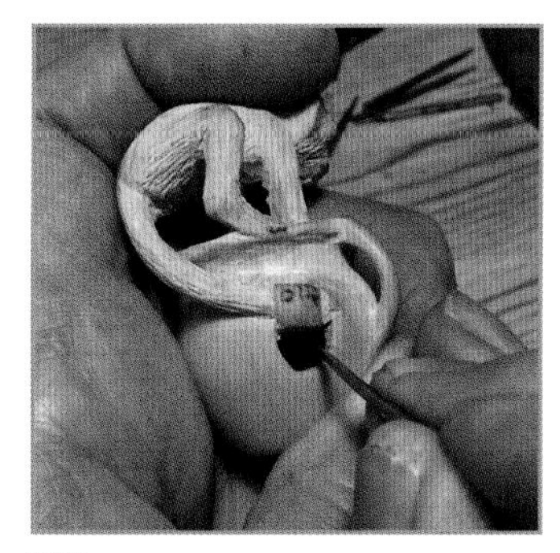

12 Having said that, scraping the sides will produce the best results. Take your time doing this as the inside of the pot is the part most people will study to find out how you have carved it.

13 When you have removed the majority of the waste, finish thinning down the monkey before adding the texture. You may be able to come back and smooth the inside of the pot even further once the limbs are thinner.

Carving the fur

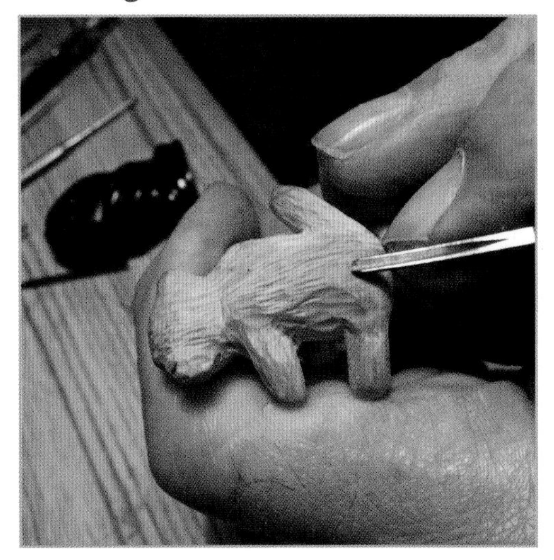

14 Follow the same process for carving the fur as shown on the rabbit project (see page 50). The only difference is that you now have several awkward areas to reach. There should be enough room to get to these, although you may need to scrape some of the more difficult bits where you cannot get a V tool in.

15 Check the direction of the hair tracts and make sure that you only cut very short lines – monkeys do not have very long fur. When you are satisfied, give the whole piece a sanding using a fine abrasive, 600 grit or finer.

Carving the hands and feet

16 When creating something this small, you cannot expect to carve detailed fingers and toes. Carve the general shape, then use V cuts to show the position of the digits. It is more important to get the overall shape right than to worry about the fine details. The eyes have been pencilled in here.

Inlaying the eyes

17 This subject has been dealt with in detail on page 43–44, so I will be brief here. Suffice to say that you will need to drill two holes, plus a fitting hole in a spare piece of timber (the same type as your carving), then make some buffalo horn dowel to fit. Once this has been fixed into the holes with high-strength adhesive, it can be trimmed, sanded down and polished.

Colouring

I used the vinegar and steel wool method of colouring on this piece, outlined in more detail on page 55. However, it does not suit every carving and you may prefer to use an alternative method.

18 Steep some fine steel wool in white vinegar for a few days, then paint it onto the monkey. The wood will turn a fairly dark grey. To darken it, dab it with a used tea bag. Leave the face untouched. Clean up any areas where the colouring has spread unintentionally with a little scraping.

19 When the piece has dried, rub it down using a very fine abrasive before coating it with Danish oil. This will change the colour of the carving to a dark, appealing brown. Finally, add a couple more coats of oil along with some vigorous buffing. Any finishing oil should give you a similar finish.

Adding the himotoshi

20 With this design it is not necessary to add a *himotoshi,* as there are several spaces that could serve the same purpose. If you wish to add one, it is best to put it on the bottom of the pot.

APPLE

This project is a fairly uncomplicated design, created using ivory sourced from pre-1925 billiard or snooker balls. Although these are not any good for larger carvings, they are ideal for netsuke. You can, of course, use another medium if you prefer.

APPLE

Toolbox

You will need the following:

Tools:

Miniature chisels
Files, saws and scrapers
Or power tools with rotary burrs

Additional:

Plasticine
Abrasive 80 grits to as fine as possible
A mask or respirator
Small pieces of ram's horn

Materials

The ivory I used for this project was sourced from pre-1925 billiard and snooker balls, which I purchased from charity shops or billiard table restorers. Ensure that the balls you use are real ivory, not made from synthetic materials. For information on how to test this and on the use of this very controversial material, refer to the section on materials on page 21.

NB: If you do not wish to use ivory, simply choose an alternative material.

SAFETY WARNING: There is a very remote possibility that substances like ivory, horn or bone may contain anthrax.

Creating the maquette

With this particular design, simply use a real apple as your pattern to work from. Although having said that, you may find it useful to reproduce the shape in plasticine to see how it looks when it is reduced in size and to test the shape of the leaf before carving it.

The shape of the apple will undoubtedly need to be adapted to fit any blemishes or cracks found in the ivory. Considering the age of the balls, you are likely to find large damaged areas, but these should not go far below the surface.

Producing the basic shape

1 Take a really good look at an apple, then try to copy its form as closely as possible, without reproducing it exactly. If you find it difficult to hold the apple while you work on it, consider gluing it to a block of wood with a good epoxy glue or a high-strength adhesive. Both of these work well, but will eventually come loose.

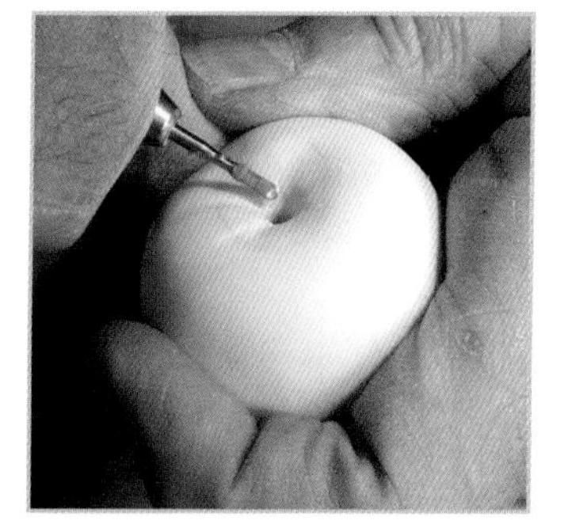

2 A simple design does not mean that you should rush the finish. On the contrary, the simpler the design, the more important the finish. It can take several hours sanding and polishing before you get the results that you are after.

TIP: Remember that the carving needs to have some sort of character. Therefore, choose an apple that has some variation in shape. Many of the modern varieties are uniform and characterless. Try to vary the surface shape and to create a softer appearance all over the piece.

Adding the insect

Having carved the apple, decide which insect you want to include, if any. You can keep it simple and just add a beetle or a ladybird, or you can get slightly more complicated and add an ant, spider or wasp.

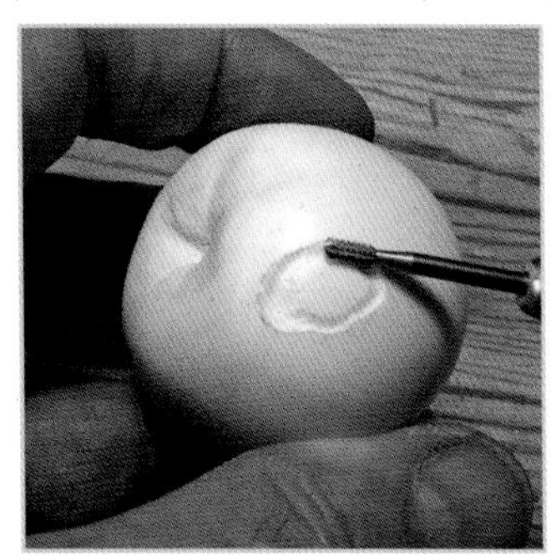

3 Whichever you choose, create a hollow and carve the insect inside it, rather than carving it separately. Rough out the hollow with a rotary burr or chisel, leaving a small lump of ivory inside it.

4 Next, draw the shape of your insect in the small hollow. In this example, I have chosen to add an ant. Refer back to research photographs to make sure that your insect is accurate. You will definitely need to use magnification to do this.

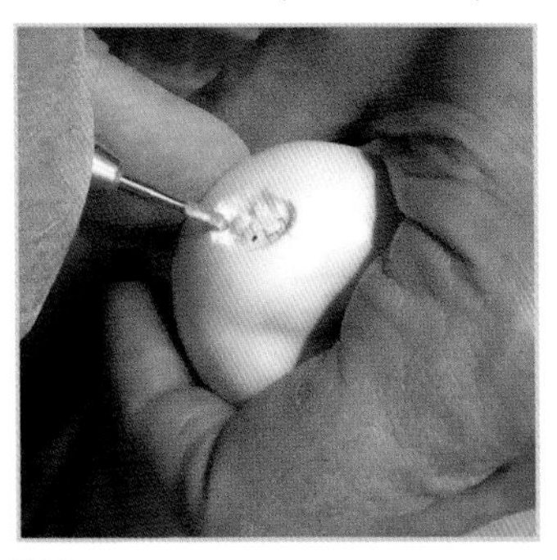

5 It is much easier to do the shaping using a fine scraper than with anything else. These shapes can be made relatively quickly from old burrs or masonry nails – for further details see page 31.

Adding additional parts

6 All that is left to do is to make the bottom floret and the stalk with its leaf. I have used ram's horn, as it can be shaped very easily using a knife or a scalpel as an alternative to power tools. For a different look, there are many attractive exotic timbers you could use.

7 Cut the horn to shape using either a coping saw or a bandsaw. The leaf will need to be shaped to suit your design. The waste that is cut off can be used to create the floret by following the same process.

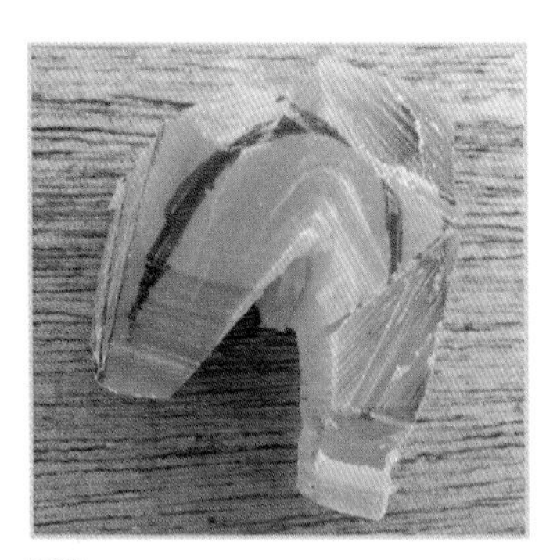

8 Something this small can be very difficult to hold while working on it. Therefore, shape the end so that it can be held in a pin vice. You will need to repeat this process when making the floret.

9 It is easier to do much of the shaping using a rotary burr. Check your reference material regularly throughout the process to ensure that the details are correct.

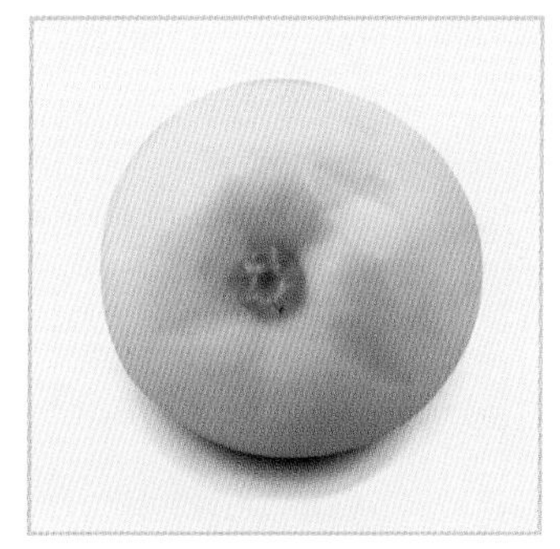

10 Polish the horn pieces with a fine felt mop in your rotary tool, using any fine polishing compound. Chrome cleaner is an inexpensive and regularly available option. Next, fit the pieces into holes at the top and bottom of the apple; these should measure around $\frac{1}{8}$in (3mm) in diameter.

Colouring the insect

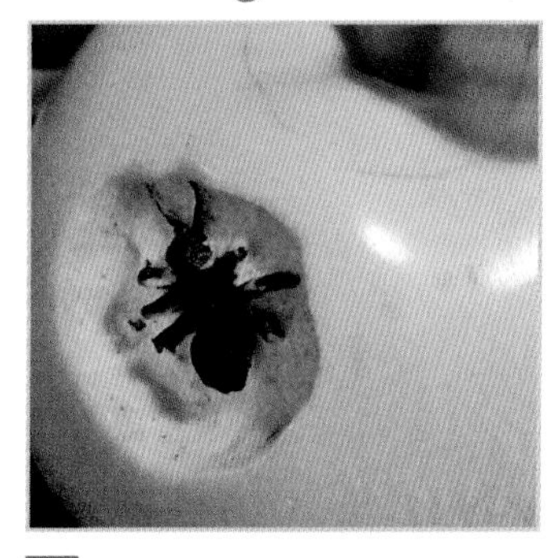

TIP: You may be slightly apprehensive at first, for when potassium is applied it will turn the insect bright purple. Practise beforehand on a spare piece of ivory.

11 Experiment with various methods of colouration. When I tried black paint and ink, the colour seemed too stark in contrast to the rest of the piece. I therefore decided to try potassium permanganate, as it produces a rich brown colour when it is dry. Make up a tiny drop of the solution and paint this onto the ant using a very small paint brush. Any surplus colour can be cleaned off with a scalpel or alternatively a scraper.

Adding the himotoshi

As I have chosen not to colour this piece, there is little to break the overall whiteness of the ivory. I added some contrast by making a feature of the *himotoshi*, which I made from a single piece of ram's horn. As the horn has a degree of translucence, the hollow underneath it needed to be darkened to add effect. You can experiment here to get the result you require. It is these variations that add to the character and individuality of each carving.

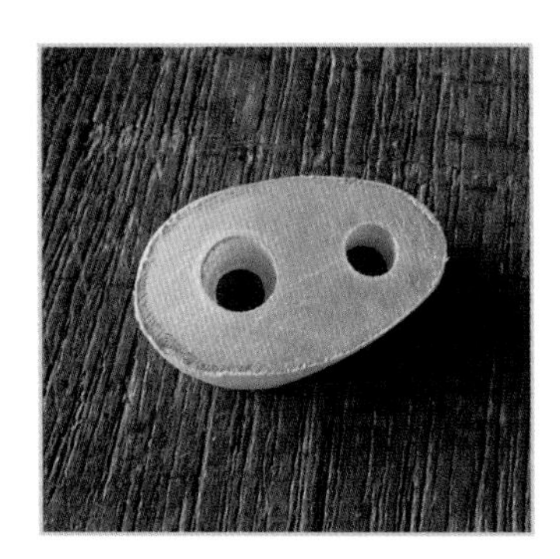

12 Cut the horn to shape using either a coping saw or a bandsaw, adding the necessary holes.

13 Lay the finished *himotoshi* on the surface of the apple and carefully scribe around it.

14 Next, carve a recess for the horn to fit in. This can be a lengthy process and should not be rushed. Keep checking for fit and be careful not to make the hole too big or you will simply have to start again.

15 Once the piece will go in neatly, paint the inside of the recess with black acrylic paint before gluing in the horn using high-strength adhesive. When the glue has set, sand the horn down, so that it is flush with the surface.

TIP: I was tempted to add colour to this piece to make it look more like a real apple, but in the end I decided that too much realism on a piece would make it appear mass produced. Besides which, ivory has its own beauty which does not require any enhancement.

Polishing

16 The apple can be polished with a variety of products - metal polish, chrome cleaner, buffing compound, even whitening toothpaste. The pieces for the horn are considerably softer, so remove the floret and the stalk before you start polishing. The best results for polishing these pieces is obtained using a fine polishing compound on a small, soft buffing wheel, after first rubbing these pieces down with a very fine abrasive (1500 grit or finer). Take care not to break or damage these pieces.

Finishing

17 Finally, glue the floret and the stalk into place with high-strength adhesive.

SNAKE

If you like the look of ivory, yet are hesitant to use it, then the tagua nut is a viable alternative. However, it is only a small nut, so size is a limitation. In addition, there is usually a void in the centre, so the design must be kept very flexible. I decided that a snake would provide the necessary flexibility and allow room for inevitable modifications along the way.

SNAKE

Toolbox

You will need the following:

If using mostly hand tools:

1/8in (3mm) number 1 or 2 chisel
1/8in (3mm) number 3
3/16in (4.5mm) number 9 gouge
Small electric drill and bits or rotary multi-tool

If using mostly motor tools:

Rotary multi-tool
Rotary burrs
Polishers and drills
Fine scrapers and chisels

NB: You may well end up using a combination of the two.

Additional:

Fabric dye
Horn for the eyes

Materials

Tagua nuts are seeds from the ivory nut palm found in the forests of South America. These seeds start off soft enough to eat, but after drying out for several months, they become extremely hard. For over a hundred years they have been used to create a wide range of products. In fact, at one time the buttons on the uniforms of the American army were made from tagua nuts. Since the widespread ban on the trading of elephant ivory has come into force, tagua nuts, with their strong resemblance to ivory, have seen a resurgence.

Creating the maquette

Each tagua nut is a slightly different shape, so your design should be based on your selected nut. Use the maquette to get the coils of the snake in as pleasing a shape as possible. Assume that you will find a void in the centre and plan accordingly. Once you have opened the nut to find the void, you will need to go back to your maquette and redesign it.

At this stage you should have a pretty good idea whether your original design can be carved using your individual tagua nut. Any adjustments that are needed should be done on the maquette first, as this is easier to change. Your finished design will inevitably differ from this maquette, so only use it to provide a general idea of what the finished piece will look like.

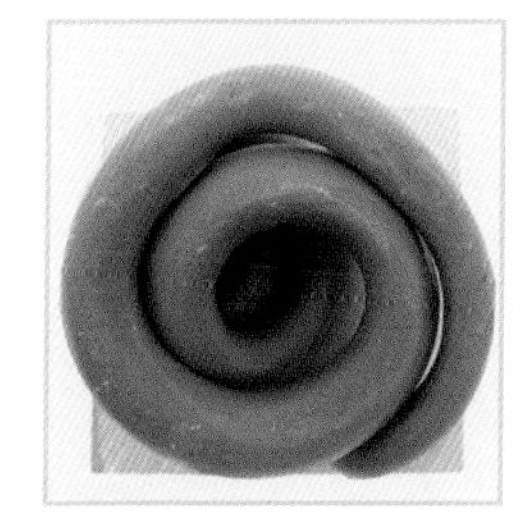

SAFETY WARNING: Always wear protective goggles. When working with tagua nuts, especially with hand tools, you will create small sharp shards of material that fly about everywhere. When these are wet they become translucent, therefore if they get into your eye they can be very difficult to find and remove.

Roughing out the figure

1 Once you have selected your nut and the design you are using for the snake, start getting rid of the brown outer husk. This will expose the white of the nut beneath.

2 One end of the nut will have a small hollow in it that will need to be dug out. Always check that the inside hollow is not too large and therefore unworkable.

3 Draw on the basic coils that you produced on your maquette. Roughly shape these, making sure that everything lines up correctly.

Rounding off the body

4 When everything lines up, begin to round off the body.

5 When your shape looks right, sand it smooth or scrape it if you prefer.

6 Do not forget to include the underside of your piece.

TIP: Remember that the body of a snake is soft and that the shape will change where it overlaps or where it sits on the ground. Take a close look at research photographs, paying particular attention to how the body shape of a snake changes.

Carving the scales

There are several different methods to add scales. The method you choose will usually depend on the tools that you have at your disposal. You may even decide that you prefer the snake smooth and do not want to add any scales. If so, skip the next part and go straight to the finishing detail and polishing.

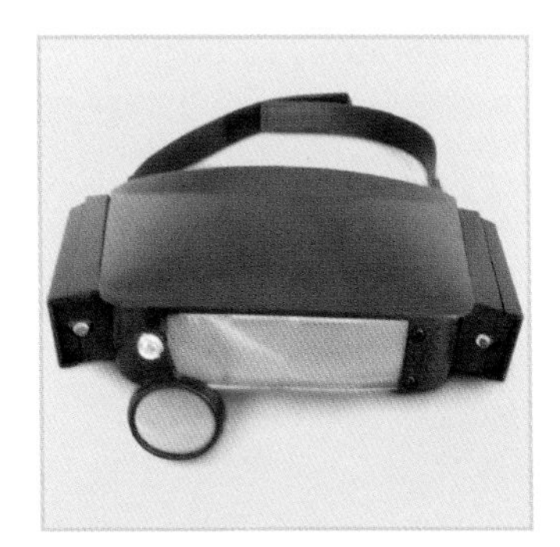

7 You will almost certainly need to use some sort of magnification to help you to see the detail of the scales.

8 Looking carefully at your research pictures of snakes, draw the scales onto your carving. Do not be tempted to carve them freehand.

9 Initially, I marked on the scales, then shaped each one individually with a rotary burr.

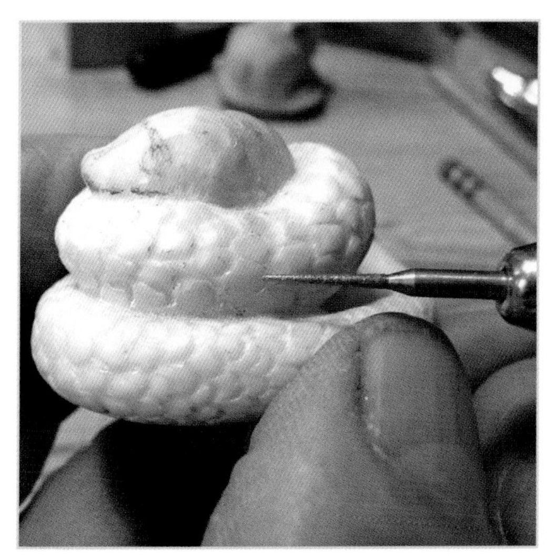

10 Carving scales individually can make them far too large and irregular. Although it requires lots of patience, it is worth taking your time marking out the lines of the scales and making sure that they are regular and evenly spaced. These scales will simply be a representation. You will not be able to carve them the correct size as they would appear far too small.

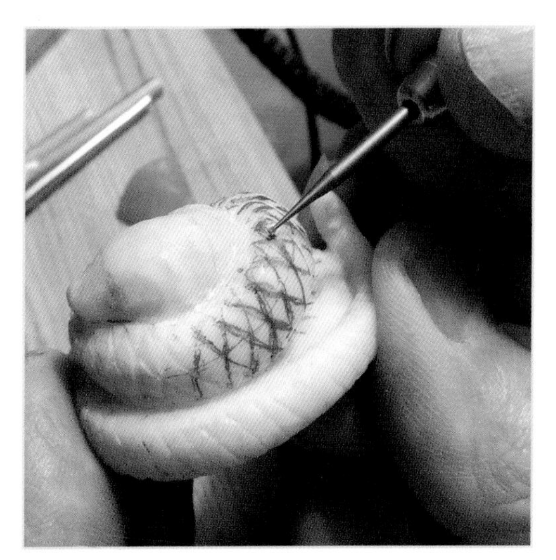

11 Having carved the scales as described in step 10, I was not satisfied, so I smoothed these down and started again using another method. The scales still formed a diagonal criss-cross pattern down the whole length of the body. Only mark these on the topside of the carving, leaving the underneath for the time being. The angle the diagonals form with each other will determine the shape of the scales.

12 The diagonal pattern was the same, just a little smaller. This time I only carved fine lines to indicate the scales with no rounding off. Cut the lines with a small wedge-shaped rotary burr – a magnifier will help you to see what you are doing more easily. Small needle file or scrapers will achieve the same results, but will take much longer. Take your time with this, as it can make or break your carving. There is also a limit to how many times you can change it.

13 Mark the scales along the underside of the snake, making sure that you maintain the pattern along its entire length. These will have a very different appearance, as they cover the muscles used for movement. They form soft ridges across the body that change shape as the snake moves along. Each line should coincide with the end of the top diagonals.

14 Use small V cuts to blend in where these bottom lines meet the top scales. If your spacing is correct they should create a neat pattern all along the edge.

TIP: There is so little written about the techniques of carving miniature pieces that much of what carvers do is trial and error – sometimes a lot more of the latter! Do not be afraid of making mistakes, even if it means having to modify your ideas or, at worst, having to accept defeat and starting again. Do not lose heart: it is all part of the learning process.

15 Fill in any cracks around the inside of your carving with either epoxy glue or white filler. You may need to experiment with both to find the best result. The one you choose will also depend on the finish that you intend to use. If you plan to colour the snake, there is no need to be quite so fussy about the colour of the filler. Having said that, check that the filler will take the colour in the same way as the tagua nut, by trying it on a spare piece beforehand. Once the glue has cured, tidy up the crevices and smooth out the curves.

Carving the head and tongue

16 Mark on the details of the head and the tongue as accurately as possible. Refer to research pictures and photographs, paying particular attention to the general body shape, as well as the details of the head.

17 Check the shape of the snake's head, especially its size in comparison to the size of its body. Snakes have very small heads, and if carved incorrectly are likely to make the whole carving look strange.

Carving the eyes

18 Once the head and the tongue are finished, drill two holes around 3/16in (1.5mm) in diameter, exactly in line with each other. Drill another hole of the same size in a spare piece of tagua for the fitting process.

19 Choose a suitable piece of ram's horn, cut it down at one end so that it fits into a pin vice. Next, scrape it into a thin cylindrical rod to the size of the fitting hole to ensure that it fits in the snake's head.

20 Carefully sand both eyes using a fine abrasive, around 8,000 grit. Polish with razor strop fungus before buffing the whole piece to a shine. Finally, check very carefully that it fits neatly into the eye socket.

21 Drop a small piece of gold leaf into the hole before applying a small drop of high-strength adhesive to the end of the rod and inserting it into the head. Carefully trim this off once it is secure. Repeat the process on the other side.

22 To add a dark pupil, drill a very fine hole in the centre of each eye into which insert a piece of black buffalo horn that has been scraped down with a scalpel.

23 When this is trimmed off and polished it gives a much better look to the eyes.

Adding the himotoshi

There is no *himotoshi* on this piece as there are already enough holes in the snake to tie a cord through. However, if you want to add one, it is best to position it underneath one of the coils. Take care when you drill as tagua nuts can be rather brittle; you may be better using a rotary burr.

Finishing

24 Polish your carving, rubbing it with your fingers for a beautiful shine. General handling will produce an appealing patina over time. If you prefer an instant effect, polish the netsuke with a wax polish.

Colouring

Add colour to your carving using Procion dyes. This is shown in detail on page 89. I diluted the dye to create a very light green, but left the underside white. I coloured the tongue using a black indelible pen.

MASK

This particular mask is centred around the material I wished to use, buffalo horn. This is often very striking, being almost jet black in colour with a certain amount of grain pattern. I searched for a subject that could make the best use of these qualities, eventually settling on a black veil draped around a woman's face made from ram's horn.

MASK

Toolbox

You will need the following:

Palm tools or block cutters:

$^{1}/_{8}$in (3mm) number 3
$^{1}/_{8}$in (3mm) number 1 or 2
$^{3}/_{16}$in (4.5mm) number 9 gouge
Dockyard chisels and gouges
Needle files or fine rifflers
Fine scrapers

Power tools:

Electric multi-tool or micromotor
Rotary burrs and polishers
Fine power saw

Additional:

Epoxy glue
Black fabric dye
Acrylic paints
Abrasive
Ram's horn

Materials

When choosing a piece of buffalo horn, be aware that there is a blood vessel or nerve running through the centre. This can spoil the finish if it remains.

In my search for a clear piece of ram's horn for the face, I had to carve three separate pieces. The first two had faults or areas of discolouration that were not evident until I started to polish the face. Unfortunately, this is the risk you take when using alternative materials to wood.

Creating the maquette

The maquette for this project will require an extensive understanding of the way the many folds around the face will lie. Before you start creating it, try wrapping various scarves around a willing female's face or, as I did, a polystyrene head. Now you can produce your maquette using the real thing, which is much more useful. Concentrate on the front view and how the fabric sits. The back of the mask does not need to be sorted at this stage, as it will depend largely on how you fit the back panel.

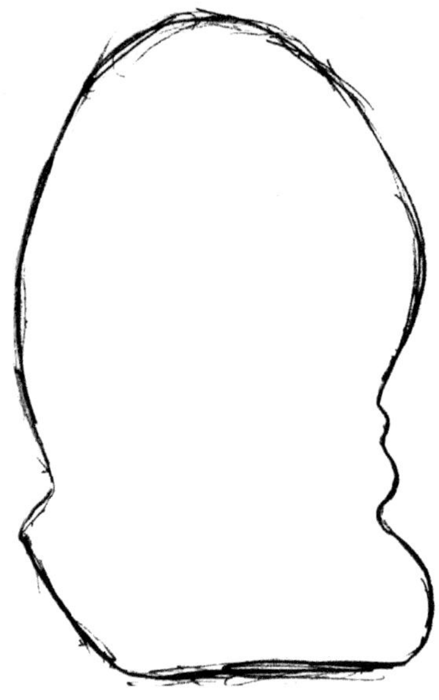

Preparation of material

1 Find a piece of buffalo horn with as little discolouration as possible. When cutting through the horn, be careful to avoid the centre line and also ensure that you have enough thickness to carve the whole piece.

2 Cut it flat on opposite sides using either a bandsaw or a hacksaw, so that you can place it on your pattern and safely cut it out on a bandsaw.

TIP: Buffalo horn varies considerably in colour as well as grain pattern. Clean up the piece that you intend to use, even polish it a little, to ensure that no undesirable grain pattern interferes with the intended design.

The pattern

3 Cut out a paper pattern from your maquette and transfer it onto the block of buffalo horn. This can be done either by sticking the paper directly onto the horn or by drawing round it with a white pencil. Cut away the waste.

4 If you are using a coping saw, instead of a bandsaw, make sure that you cut at right angles to the surface in order to achieve an accurate shape.

5 This should leave you with a block of buffalo horn the same shape as your pattern.

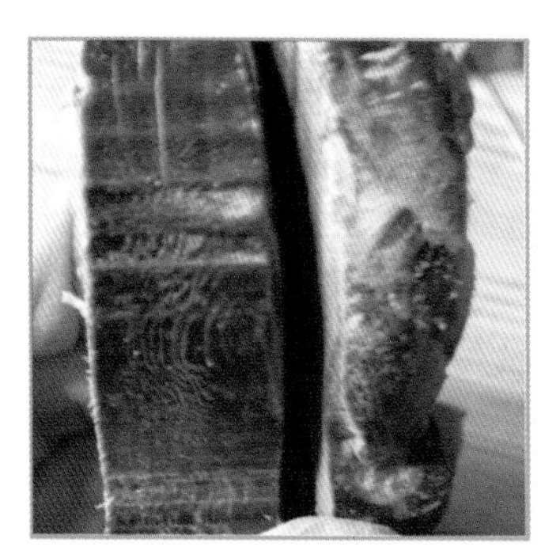

6 Cut the block into two, approximately halfway between the flat surfaces. Take care to make the cut as clean and as straight as possible.

7 Buffalo horn often has a small hole through the centre where a nerve or a blood vessel was located. In my piece, I cut through this to avoid any surface imperfections. I decided that these would probably disappear when I fitted the back, so no further action needed to be taken.

Shaping

8 The next step is to shape the main body of the mask. Remember to allow materials for the fold. Start introducing the folds with either a rotary burr or a sharp knife.

9 Then, mark the lines of the fold as shown on your maquette or on your model.

10 The recesses formed by the folds can be cut with a chisel or a small V tool (or rotary burr if you prefer).

Fitting and shaping the face

11 Cut out the opening for the face. Drill a series of holes through the buffalo horn with a small drill. Match the shape of the opening to the original model, ensuring that the folds fit naturally to the opening.

12 Use plasticine to create a pattern of the face. Shape the inside of the opening to fit the face with a recess in the front of the opening to accommodate the nose.

13 Select a piece of ram's horn, cutting off a block large enough to fit the hole. Always check it thoroughly for imperfections.

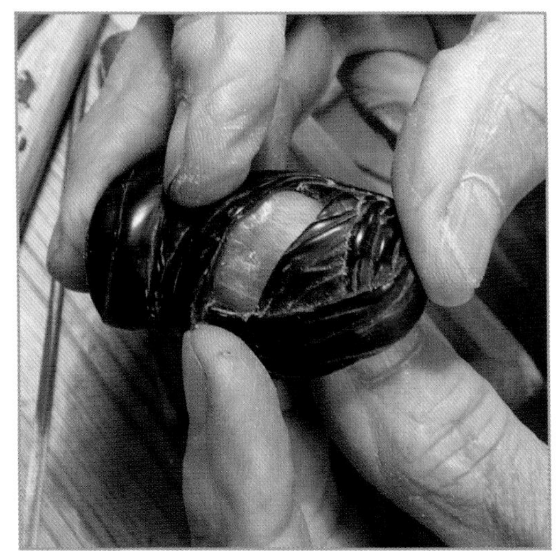

14 Replicate the plasticine pattern using the ram's horn. This is very time consuming and will need considerable care in order to achieve a good fit. You will only be able to take off very small pieces each time, so do not rush your work.

15 Draw on the profile of the face. You do not need to carve the eyes at this stage, as they do not affect the fit. Having said that, ensure that the nose fits snugly into the bottom of the veil.

TIP: You will need to offer up the face into the recess several times in order to establish where any high spots occur. If you use a soft pencil on the inside of the recess, it will mark the horn at any of these high spots and you can reduce them accordingly. Remember that the nose will protrude from the face, therefore you will need to make an equivalent shape in the centre of the lower part of the recess or the finished article will not look realistic.

Fitting the back

16 Cut a recess in the back of around 3mm (1/18in). Match up the lines to fit with the drapery you are intending to carve.

17 Create a pattern of the outline for the back plate by pressing paper into the back of your block. Cut this to the size of the inside of the recess.

18 Stick this onto the piece of buffalo horn that you cut off the original block. Cut the back to size before fitting it into the recess.

19 By marking the edges with a white pencil and pressing the two pieces together, any high spots become evident. You can reduce these by scraping with a knife or a fine file, although it is a lengthy process.

TIP: You may find it easier to stick the two halves together with hot melt glue while sanding them. The glue is strong enough to hold the two pieces together while you are working, but means they can be easily separated when you have finished.

Drapery on the back

20 When you have a good fit, mark on the lines of drapery that you are putting on the back. By making the recesses of the folds coincide with the join lines, these lines should not be too evident in the finished piece.

21 Cut in the drapery detail, then sand it down to achieve continuous lines going from the front around to the back. Take your time with this, as it will make all the difference to the result.

Detailing the face

TIP: Mount the face onto a piece of spare wood. Something this small can be awkward to hold, and if you are working with rotary tools the cutting parts can come dangerously close to your fingertips.

22 Carving the eyes and the bridge of the nose is another lengthy process. I strongly recommend experimenting on a spare piece of horn beforehand.

The eyes

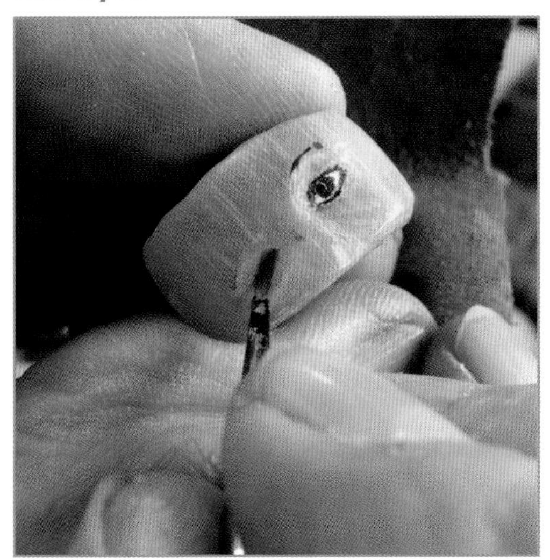

23 Paint the eyes on the face using acrylics for the white and the iris. Use Indian ink for the lashes and eyebrows. Apply both with the aid of a very small brush. You may need to do this more than once to get the effect you require. However, remember that the piece only needs a very subtle colouring. Too much colour will make it appear garish.

Polishing and fixing the face and the back

24 Next, line the inside of the opening with glue before pressing in the face. Make sure that it is a snug fit.

25 Once this has set, do the same thing with the back before leaving them both for a day or so to ensure everything cures thoroughly.

TIP: When using glue with buffalo horn, mix a minute quantity of super black polyester dye with the clear epoxy glue. This does a great job of hiding most of the join lines - refer to the suppliers list on page 158. Be careful not to use too much glue, as it is difficult to clean it off the finished face. If excess glue is evident, it is much easier to clean it off when it has thoroughly set.

Adding the himotoshi

26 Drill the back for the *himotoshi*. This is best done in the part below the backplate, as this is the area that has the most material. If you go any higher you run the risk of going right through the back into the cavity beneath. A ball-shaped burr will clean out the holes and provide a neat finish for polishing.

Finishing

27 Clean off any surplus glue, then start the final rubbing down and polishing. Go through the grades of abrasive right down to 12,000 grit. Going all over the piece with Razor strop fungus will also bring up a beautiful finish.

28 Any gaps or imperfections that appear after the sanding has been finished can be filled in using stained epoxy glue and the piece re-sanded. Finally, buff the whole netsuke with your fingers followed by a soft polishing cloth.

SAFETY WARNING: There are three main points to bear in mind when working with materials like buffalo or ram's horn. Firstly, if you are using power to grind or polish, ALWAYS wear a mask. Secondly, it is very easy to scratch the surface when cleaning off any imperfections. This results in white marks that can spoil the finish. Take great care at this stage to keep both the surface and the creases absolutely smooth. Finally, if you are using power tools to polish, avoid excess pressure as it is easy to overheat the horn or to create scratch marks which cannot be removed. Your patience will be well rewarded.

GALLERY

Gallery

The following pages showcase the exceptional work of netsuke carvers, from relative newcomers to world-renowned experts.

Clive Hallam

Clive is amongst the world's top professional netsuke carvers. He is a British artist who spent many years intensively studying Japanese netsuke techniques. The quality of his work is such that, on completion, it is instantly acquired by major international collections. In the piece below, the log, 38mm in length, is carved from rare fossilized *umimatsu*, with inlays created from stained boar tusk and horn. It is shown from various angles to illustrate how intricate and delicate Clive's work is.

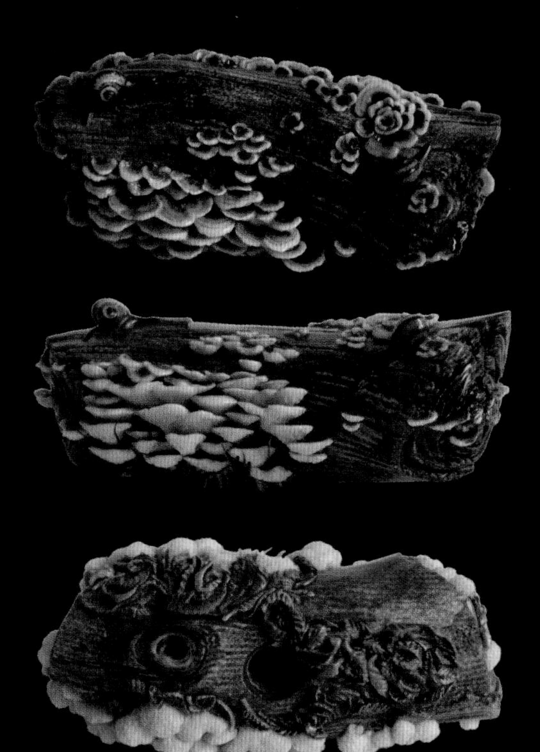

Below are further examples of the author's work, carved from a variety of materials.

Old man asleep over his book

In my hectic life, I wanted to depict calm and quiet. Carved from an antique ivory snooker ball.

Old lady with straw hat

As well as the straw hat, all sorts of clothing textures have been added to this piece. Carved from an antique ivory snooker ball.

Chimp and termite mound

Designed to illustrate how chimps use tools to get termites out of their mound to eat them. Carved in boxwood, eyes inlaid in buffalo horn with a natural finish.

Foxes exploring dustbin

This is based on what we know goes on but seldom see. Carved in boxwood with buffalo horn eyes. It is coloured with both fabric dye and with vinegar and wire wool.

Boy doing a backwards roll

This piece was made to mark more than 30 years teaching small boys gymnastics. Carved from an ivory snooker ball.

Polar bear

The first (and only, so far) netsuke carved by 'Em'. It is carved in soft basswood with it's eyes and nose made from buffalo horn.

Peabody Essex Museum

The museum houses contributions from many of America's most important collections of 19th- and 20th-century Japanese art, illuminating the varied art and culture of Japan. It holds many rare works, considered so even in Japan, with the museum's late Edo- and Meiji-period collection ranking among the finest in the world.

The *Kirin*, a mythical beast

Couple having tea

Bag of grain with rats

Buddha sculpture

Snake in a pumpkin

Demon mask

Sounding horn

***Otafuku* sitting in the demon mask**

Carp among the waves

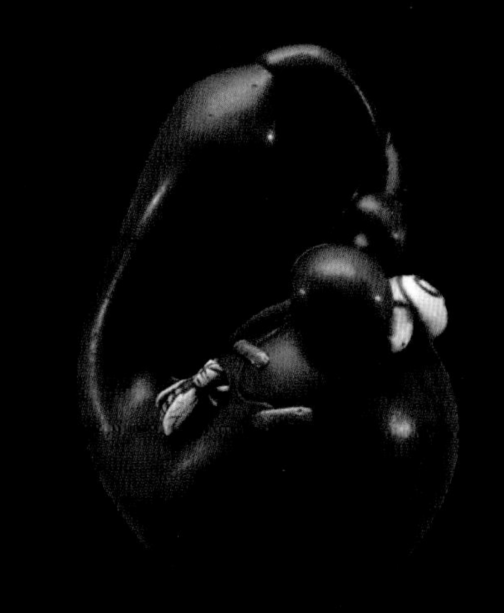

Insects on a gourd

Crouching rabbit

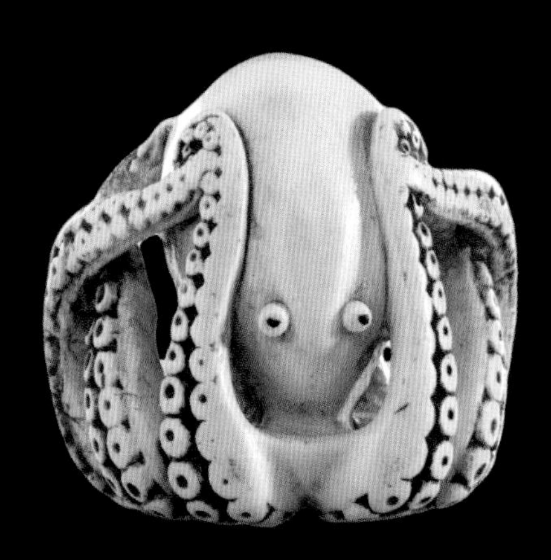

Octopus

Michael Webb

Michael was one of the very first professional netsuke carvers outside Japan since the 19th century. Although he is no longer carving, his work remains highly admired. Netsuke enthusiasts are particularly impressed by his realistic depiction of animals and birds. His netsuke are true three-dimensional sculptures – turn any one of them round in your hand and you will find a new visual delight from every angle. The majority of Michael's netsuke were carved in boxwood and many were coloured by immersing them in hot-water fabric dye, masking off different areas with latex to attain varied effects. Contrasting colours and the use of other materials, such as buffalo horn, further highlight the fine details.

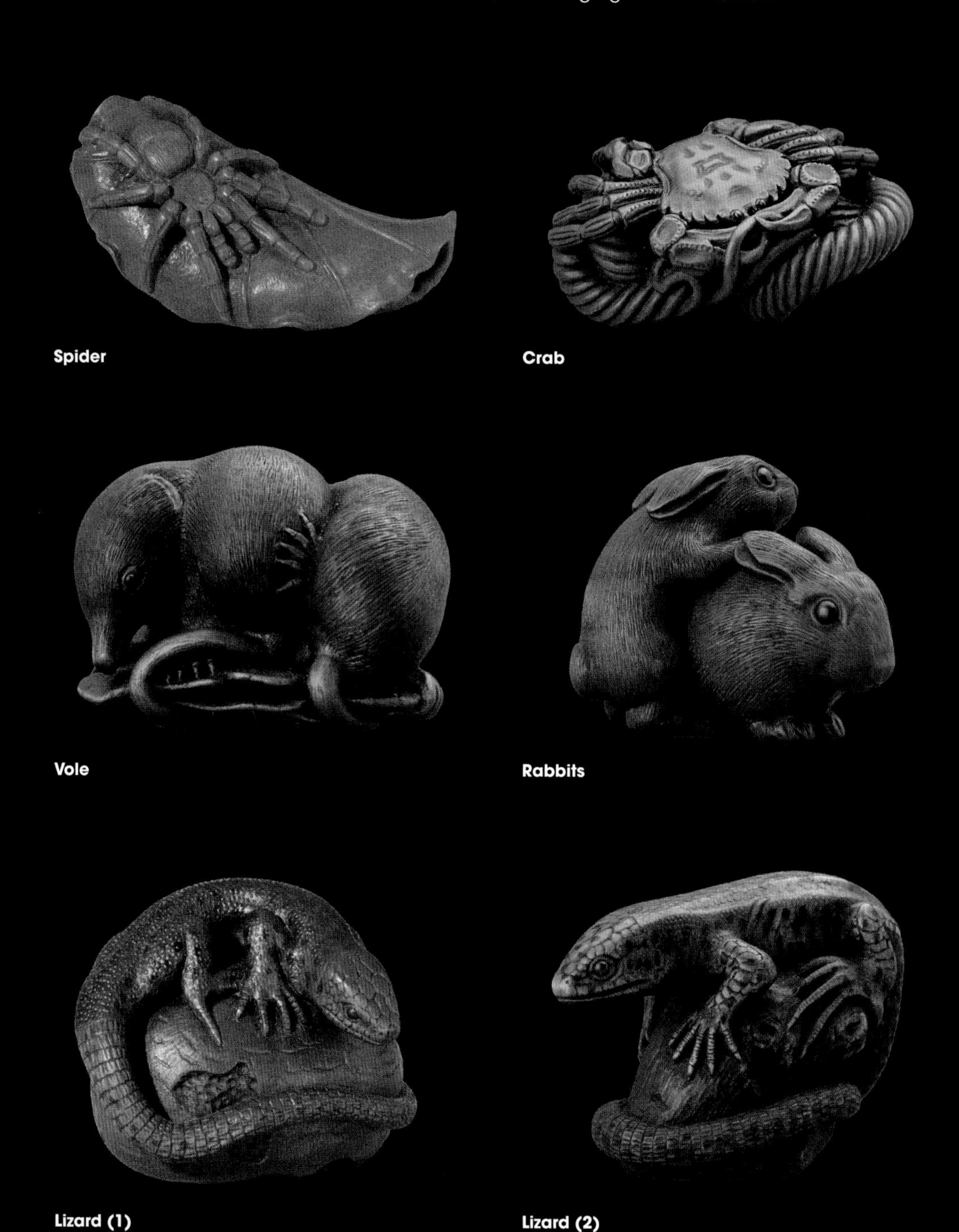

Spider

Crab

Vole

Rabbits

Lizard (1)

Lizard (2)

Russell Birch

Relative newcomer to the world of netsuke carving, Russell only began carving in the late 90s. After acquiring a few basic tools he carved his first piece; and then there was no turning back. With the help of Peter Benson and Clive Hallam he has concentrated on carving netsuke, not only from wood, but also buffalo horn, hippopotamus tusk, stag antler and many other materials.

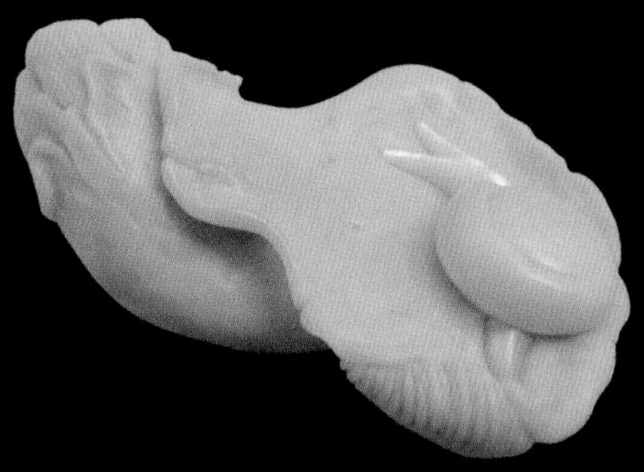

Snail on oyster mushroom

Oyster mushroom and snail shell carved from hippopotamus tusk. Snail's body inlaid with mother of pearl.

Catfish

Carved from hippopotamus tusk, amber eyes inlaid with a gold foil backing.

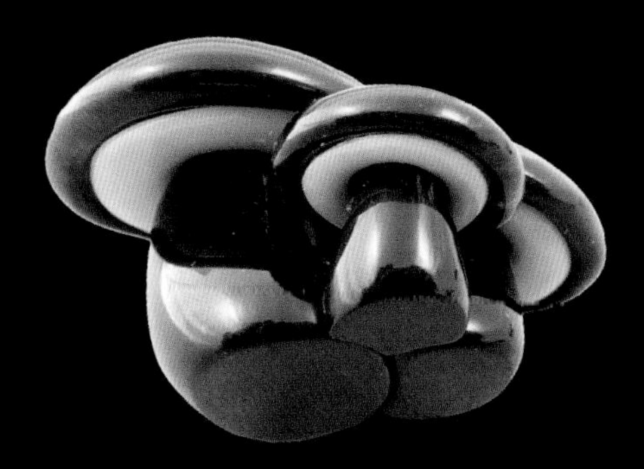

Group of mushrooms

Nine individual pieces carved from buffalo horn and tagua nut. All nine pieces are then pinned together.

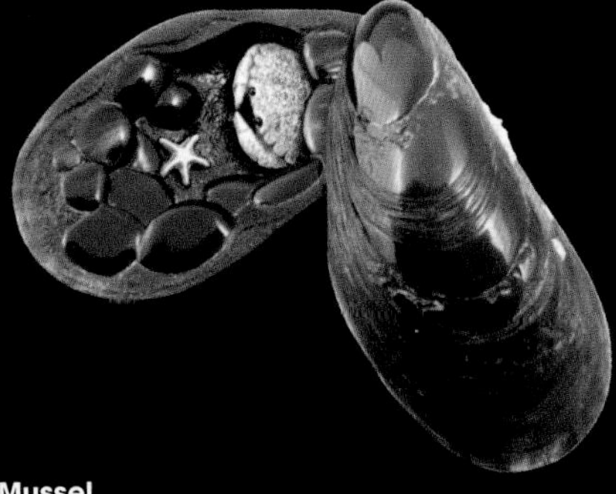

Mussel

Shells carved from buffalo horn; barnacles, crab and stingray from hippopotamus tusk. The starfish from mother of pearl.

Owl in tree

Carved from stag antler and umimatsu, the eyes on the owl and the lizard are inlaid amber and the leaves are mother of pearl.

Snail on fungi

Carved from lemon wood, the complete carving was delicately stained using different dyes.

Susan Wraight

Susan is one of the top non-Japanese netsuke carvers in the world today. Over the last 29 years, major exhibitions of her work have been held worldwide. Collections containing examples of her work include those of H I H Prince Takamado of Japan, The Kyoto Seishu Netsuke Art Museum, and the White House. Susan was recently awarded the Golden Dragon Award by the Kinsey International Art Foundation for her work. 'My work is a celebration, an acclamation of all that delights and intrigues me and of those experiences that mark my artistic journey... My imagery is drawn largely from the natural world.'

Furoshiki

Designed to celebrate the life of the late H I H Prince Takamado of Japan. His patronage of netsuke worldwide was a wonderful gift of encouragement to all netsuke carvers, so the netsuke is shown as a gift wrapped in a traditional Japanese furoshiki cloth. The parcel is round, symbolizing completeness, while the covering of the cloth alludes to a shroud. The Monarch butterfly is a symbol of the prince and his royal lineage.

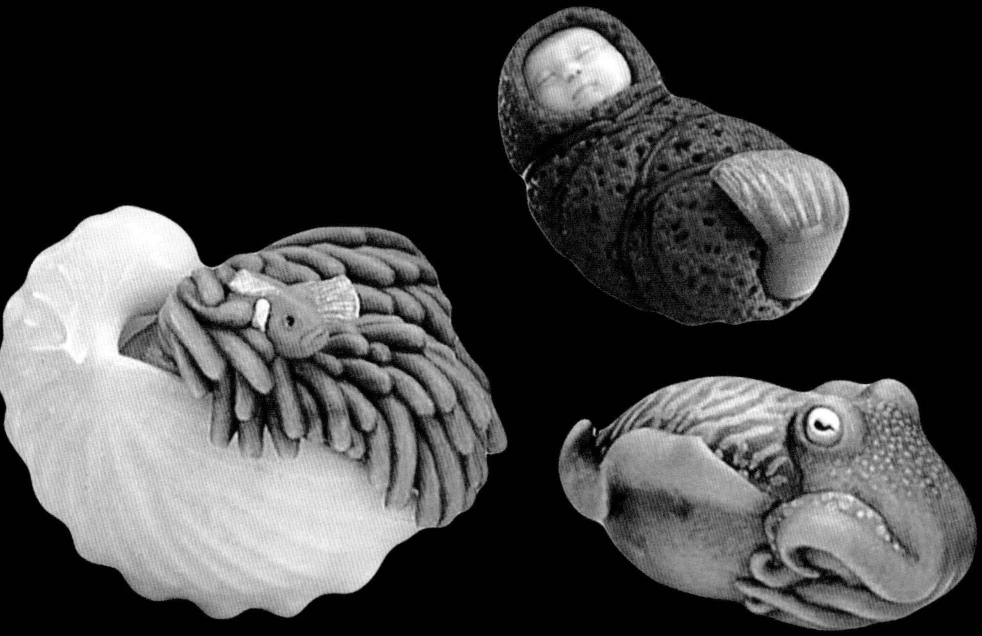

Cradle

This piece has a choice of three inserts that fit into the shell to make a complete netsuke. The title refers to the way in which the ocean is the source of life, nurturing and sustaining a diversity of creatures. It also has a rich place in our cultural heritage. Cradle is one of a series of works designed to encourage us to protect the fragile marine environment. It is carved from a variety of materials: boxwood, tagua nut, pink ivorywood, with inlays of mother of pearl and amber over gold leaf.

Belling the cat

One of a series carved to illustrate Aesop's well-known fables. Carved in boxwood. The eyes of the mice are inlaid with buffalo horn; the eye of cat is amber over gold leaf. Finished with an 18ct gold bell.

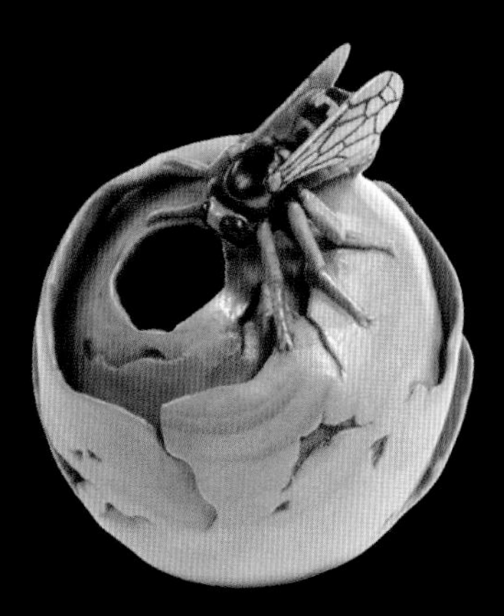

Paper palace

In the delicate structure of the wasp's beautiful, but fragile nest the queen wasp's entire colony is raised. This carving was made to comment on the ephemeral nature of material things. Carved in boxwood.

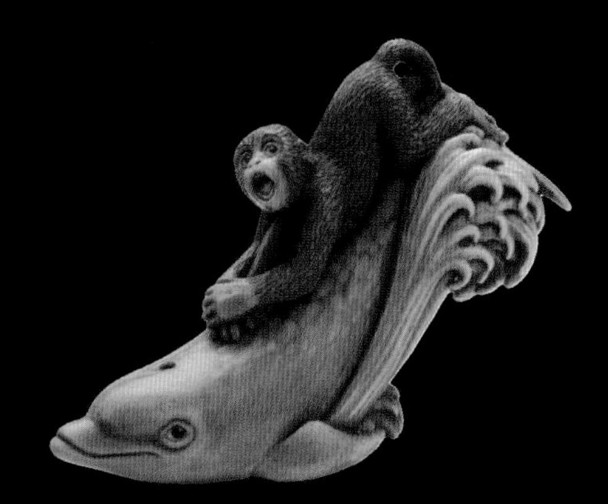

Monkey and dolphin

An illustration of another of Aesop's fables. This shows the moment when the dolphin has realized that the monkey is an impostor and is diving down beneath the waves. Carved in boxwood with inlaid buffalo horn for the eyes.

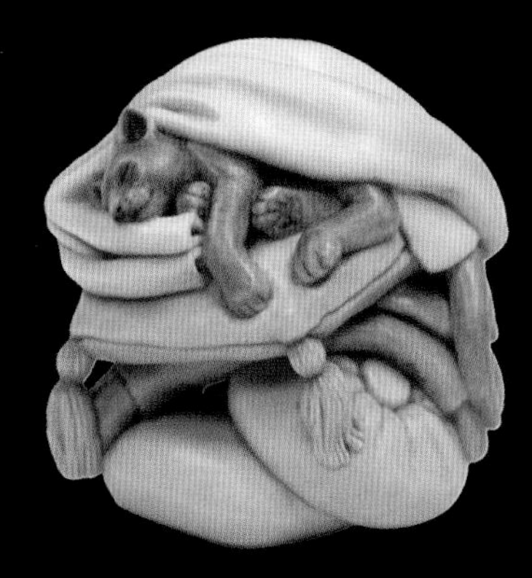

Princess and the pea

This netsuke is an adaptation of Hans Christian Andersen's much-loved tale. The cat has fallen blissfully asleep on the cushions that have been tossed to the floor by the Princess as she tries, in vain, to sleep. Carved in boxwood.

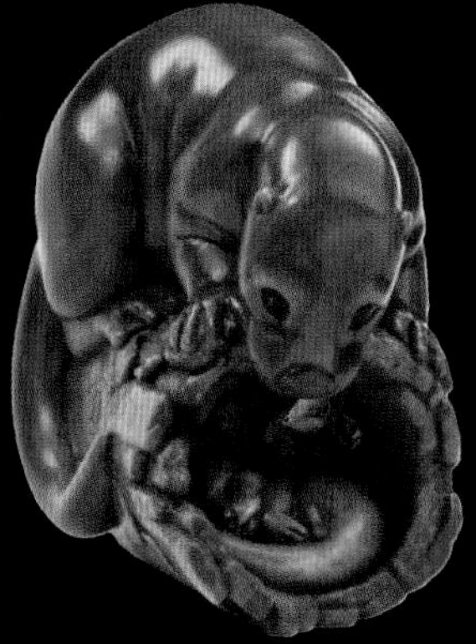

Lost and found

This otter has gone in search of her lost cub only to find him fast asleep in a rotten log, exhausted by play. Carved in boxwood with inlaid buffalo horn for the eyes.

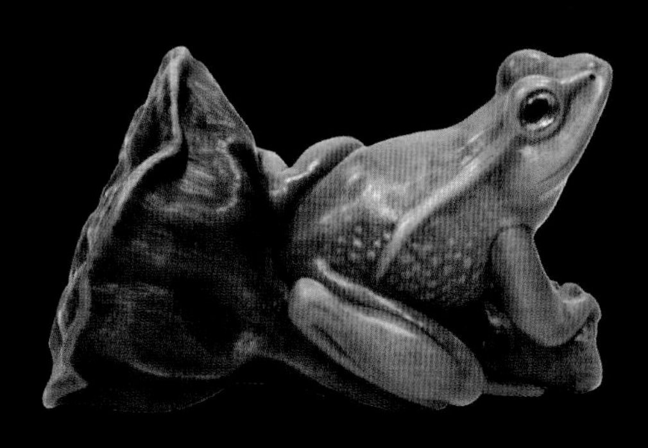

Frog on a lotus pod

The seeds of the lotus pod rattle within their sockets, adding sound to the properties of this piece. Carved in boxwood and buffalo horn with amber inlaid over gold leaf for the frog's eyes.

SUPPLIERS

UK

Carving tools

Ashley Iles
+ 44 (0)1790 763 372
www.ashleyiles.turningtools.co.uk

Classic Hand Tools
+ 44 (0)1473 784 983
www.classichandtools.co.uk

Henry Taylor Tools
+ 44 (0)1142 340 282
www.henrytaylortools.co.uk

Workshop Heaven Fine Tools
+ 44 (0)1295 780 003
www.workshopheaven.com

General sculpture and craft equipment

(Including polyester pigments)

Alec Tiranti
+ 44 (0)845 123 2100
www.tiranti.co.uk

Ivory antler and horn

Highlandhorn
+ 44 (0)1381 622 488
www.highlandhorn.com

Micromotors

Dentalvital
+ 44 (0)121 354 4969
www.dentalvital.co.uk

Power tools, burrs and accessories

Shesto
+ 44 (0)20 8451 6188
www.shesto.co.uk
(Also stocks magnifiers and micromotors)

Sutton Tools
www.suttontools.co.uk
(Also stocks magnifiers and abrasives)

Timber and other materials

Limehouse Timber
+ 44 (0)1702 469 292

Lincolshire Woodcraft Supplies
+ 44 (0)1780 757 825
www.lincolnshirewoodcraft.co.uk

Snainton Woodworking Supplies
+ 44 (0)1723 859 545
www.snaintonwoodturning.co.uk

The Wood Store
+ 44 (0)1273 570 500
www.woodrecycling.org.uk

Timberline
+ 44 (0)1732 355 626
www.exotichardwoods.co.uk

Wessex Timber
+ 44 (0)1452 740 610
www.wessextimber.co.uk

US and Canada

Amber

Ambericawest

www.ambericawest.com

Carving tools

MDI Woodcarvers Supply

800-866-5728 (Toll free)

www.mdiwoodcarvers.com

Smokey Mountain Woodcarvers Supply

800-541-5994 (Toll free)

www.woodcarvers.com

The Tool Box

432-553-5996

www.thecarverstoolbox.com

The Woodcraft Shop

800-397-2278 (Toll free)

www.thewoodcraftshop.com

Woodcraft

800-225-1153 (Toll free)

www.woodcraft.com

Ivory antler and horn

Boonetrading

1-800-796-4511 (Toll free)

www.boonetrading.com

Kowakivory

907-479-9335 (May to September)

520-207-6620 (October to April)

www.kowakivory.com

Power tools, burrs and accessories

Chipping Away

519-743-9008

www.chippingaway.com

Foredom

203-792-8622

www.foredom.com

Tools for working wood

718-499-5877

www.toolsforworkingwood.com

GLOSSARY

Buffalo horn From the water buffalo. It can be any colour from jet black to almost translucent.

Himotoshi The two small holes underneath or at the back of a netsuke carving, to take the fine cord from the *sagemono* or the *inro*.

Inro A case of several individual compartments used to hold valuables. Usually finished with decorative lacquer.

Katabori A netsuke that has every facet carved, including the underneath.

Kimono The traditional Japanese dress worn by both men and women.

Manju The oldest type of netsuke, usually round and flat.

Mask Netsuke carved in the shape of a mask.

Micromotor A high-speed rotary tool with the motor in the handpiece. This runs virtually vibration free.

Netsuke A carved toggle attached to the end of a fine cord holding the *inro* or *sagemono* in place.

Netsuke-shi The Japanese netsuke artists.

Obi The sash worn around the waist over the traditional kimono.

Ojime The bead on the cord above the *inro* used to hold the box shut. This can be plain or intricately carved.

Procion dye A very concentrated fabric dye that can be used to colour netsuke.

Ram's horn The horn from either a ram or horned sheep.

Razor strop fungus A fungus that is found on dying silver-birch trees and used as an abrasive.

Rotary burr Tungsten carbide cutters of varying shapes to fit in a rotary power tool.

Sagemono A case for valuable objects. Similar to the *inro*, but with only one compartment.

Sashi A long, thin netsuke that is tucked into the top of the *obi*.

Shibayama An old Japanese art form, the art of semiprecious inlays on lacquer.

Stop cut A safety cut that is made at right angles to the direction of cut to prevent the knife or chisel from shooting out of control.

Ukibori The process of making small raised areas or bumps on your carving.

Umimatsu Fossilized coral used for carving or decoration.

V tool Any tool that will cut a V section in the wood. Useful for lettering or for carving hair or fur.

Veiner A small number 9 gouge with extended sides, useful for getting deep into the wood.

BIBLIOGRAPHY

Bandini. R., *Expressions of Style – Netsuke as Art,* Scholten Japanese Art, 2001

Bernard, H., *Masterpieces of Netsuke Art: One Thousand Favorites of Leading Collectors,* International Netsuke Collect Society/ Weatherhill, 1973

Bushell, R., *Collectors Netsuke,* Weatherhill, 1971

Bushell, R., *Netsuke: Familiar and Unfamiliar,* Weatherhill, 1975

Bushell, R. & Masotoshi, N., *The Art of Netsuke Carving,* Weatherhill, 1992

Bushell, R., *The Wonderful World of Netsuke,* Tuttle Publishing, 1995

Earle, J., *An Introduction to Netsuke,* Her Majesty's Stationery Office, 1982

Earle, J., *Netsuke: Fantasy and Reality in Japanese Miniature Sculpture,* Museum of Fine Arts, 2004

Hutt, J., *Japanese Netsuke,* Victoria and Albert Museum, 2003

Kinsey, M., *Contemporary Netsuke,* Tuttle Publishing, 1977

Miriam, K., *Living Masters of Netsuke,* Kodansha America, 1984

Putney, C. M., *Japanese Treasures – The Art of Netsuke Carving,* The Toledo Museum of Art, 2000

Sandfield, N., Shelton, H., *Ichiro: Master Netsuke Carver,* Shelton Family Press, 2009

Symmes, Jr. E., *Netsuke: Japanese Life and Legend in Miniature,* Tuttle Publishing, 2000

Websites

For more information on miniature carving and netsuke pieces visit:

Guy Shaw
www.forestdeer.ndo.co.uk

Janel Jacobson
www.janeljacobson.com

Leigh Sloggett
www.leighsloggett.com

Netsuke Online Research Centre
www.netsukeonline.org

Peabody Essex Museum
www.pem.org

Sergey Osipov
www.osipovnetsuke.com

The Carving Path
www.thecarvingpath.net/forum

The International Netsuke Society
www.netsuke.org

The World of Netsuke
www.world-of-netsuke.com

Victoria and Albert Museum
www.VAM.AC.uk

ABOUT THE AUTHOR

Peter Benson started woodcarving as a hobby back in 1947. His particular interest is miniature netsuke carvings. At the other end of the scale is the two-ton, full-sized polar bear he helped to create as a memorial to the 49th Infantry Division of the British Army. Since his retirement from full-time employment, Peter has taken his interest to a new level, setting up the Essex School of Woodcarving to provide courses for carvers of all abilities, as well as teaching woodcarving skills throughout America, Canada, France and Australia. In addition to his teaching commitments abroad, Peter has a full schedule in the UK travelling the length and breadth of the country conducting workshops or talks and judging various competitions. Peter firmly believes that anyone can carve given the right approach and guidance, and that it should always be a fun experience.

ACKNOWLEDGEMENTS

When producing your first book, a great deal is owed to the people who offer help, encouragement and support. I would particularly like to thank the following:

Mark Baker from GMC, who first encouraged me to write this book and has supported me throughout. Beth Wicks, without whom this book would never have happened. She has kept me on target through all the difficulties that have arisen, being critical, persuasive and urgent in the nicest possible way. That this book has been published is almost entirely due to her efforts in dealing with me.

Michael Webb, for encouraging me in the very early days and for providing me with so much helpful information and guidance that it stays with me still. Rosemary Bandini, for agreeing to let me use pictures of Michael's work and to his family for supplying them. The Peabody Essex Museum in Salem, Massachusetts, for supplying images from their fantastic collection.

Sue Wraight for supplying me with such a wonderful selection of pictures of her netsuke for the gallery section. Her amazing work continues to inspire and motivate me. Clive Hallam for sharing his vast knowledge of materials and techniques and for allowing me to use the pictures of his latest masterpiece. Pictures of his work are rarely seen and I consider this a real privilege. Russell Birch for taking in every word of advice he is given and using it to produce yet another beautiful carving. Each new piece is an encouragement to anyone wanting to carve small pieces.

Finally, and most importantly, Marlene, 'Em', who has put up with being ignored for long periods of time, has suffered my tensions and worries and the mess around the house from my carvings, as well as the reams of paper liberally scattered. Without her support and encouragement the whole project would have been abandoned in the very early stages and I might well be living on my lonesome.

PICTURE CREDITS

Step-by-step photography by Peter and 'Em' Benson, also on page 151.

All other photography by Anthony Bailey, except those below:

Russell Birch: pages 10 and 155
Adam Carter: page 13
Clive Hallam: page 150
Mark Sexton, courtesy of the Peabody Essex Museum: pages 152–3
Luigi Bandini: page 154
Susan Wraight: pages 156–7

INDEX

S

T

U

V

W

To place an order, or to request a catalogue, contact:

GMC Publications Ltd

Castle Place, 166 High Street, Lewes, East Sussex, BN7 1XU United Kingdom

Tel: + 44 (0) 1273 488005 Fax: + 44 (0) 1273 402866 Website: www.gmcbooks.com